Conversations with Edna O'Brien

Literary Conversations Series
Peggy Whitman Prenshaw
General Editor

Conversations
with Edna O'Brien

Edited by Alice Hughes Kersnowski

University Press of Mississippi   *Jackson*

www.upress.state.ms.us

The University Press of Mississippi is a member
of the Association of American University Presses.

First printing 2014

∞

Library of Congress Cataloging-in-Publication Data

Conversations with Edna O'Brien / edited by Alice Hughes Kersnowski.
    pages cm. — (Literary Conversations Series)
  Includes index.
  ISBN 978-1-61703-872-3 (cloth : alk. paper) — ISBN 978-1-61703-873-0 (ebook) 1.
O'Brien, Edna—Interviews. 2. Authors, Irish—20th century—Interviews. I. Kers-
nowski, Alice Hughes, editor of compilation.
  PR6065.B7Z66 2014
  823'.914—dc23
  [B]   2013018593

British Library Cataloging-in-Publication Data available

Selected Published Works by Edna O'Brien

Novels:
The Country Girls. London: Hutchinson, 1960.
The Lonely Girl. (republished as *Girl with Green Eyes*). London: Cape, 1962 (1964).
Girls in Their Married Bliss. London: Cape, 1964.
August Is a Wicked Month. London: Cape, 1965.
Casualties of Peace. London: Cape, 1966.
A Pagan Place. London: Weidenfeld & Nicolson, 1970.
Night. London: Weidenfeld & Nicolson, 1972.
Johnny, I Hardly Knew You. London: Weidenfeld & Nicolson, 1977.
The Country Girls Trilogy, Omnibus Edition. London: Cape, 1987.
The High Road. London: Weidenfeld & Nicolson, 1988.
Time and Tide. New York: Viking. 1992.
House of Splendid Isolation. London: Weidenfeld & Nicolson, 1994.
Down by the River. London: Weidenfeld & Nicolson, 1996.
Wild Decembers. London: Weidenfeld & Nicolson, 1999.
In the Forest. London: Weidenfeld & Nicolson, 2002.
The Light of Evening. London: Weidenfeld & Nicolson, 2006.

Collections of Short Stories:
The Love Object. London: Cape, 1968.
A Scandalous Woman: Stories. London: Weidenfeld & Nicolson, 1974.
Mrs Reinhardt and Other Stories. London: Weidenfeld & Nicolson, 1978.
The Collected Edna O'Brien. London: Collins, 1978.
Returning: Tales. London: Weidenfeld & Nicolson, 1982.
A Fanatic Heart: Selected Stories. London: Weidenfeld & Nicolson, 1985.
Lantern Slides: Short Stories. London: Weidenfeld & Nicolson, 1990.
Love's Lesson. London: Cuckoo Press, 2000.
Saints and Sinners. London: Faber and Faber, 2011.

Stage Plays:
A Cheap Bunch of Nice Flowers. Plays of the Year Vol. 26. London: Elek, 1963.
Zee & Co. London: Weidenfeld & Nicolson, 1971.
A Pagan Place: A Play. London: Faber & Faber, 1973.
Virginia: A Play. London: Hogarth Press, 1981.
Iphigenia [of] Euripides. London: Methuen, 2003.
Triptych and Iphigenia: Two Plays New York, Grove Press, 2005.
Haunted. London: Faber and Faber, 2010.
Screenplays:
Girl with Green Eyes. United Artists Corporation: 1964.
I Was Happy Here. The Rank Organisation: 1966.
X, Y, and Zee. Columbia Pictures: 1972.
The Country Girls: London Film Productions: 1984.

Nonfiction:
Mother Ireland. London: Weidenfeld & Nicolson, 1976.
Arabian Days. London: Quartet, 1977.
James and Nora: A Portrait of Joyce's Marriage. London: Lord John Press, 1981.
Vanishing Ireland. London: Cape, 1986.
James Joyce. London: Weidenfeld & Nicolson, 1999.
Byron in Love: A Short Daring Life. London: Weidenfeld & Nicolson, 2009.
Country Girl: A Memoir. London: Faber and Faber, 2012.

Children's Stories:
The Dazzle. London: Hodder & Stoughton, 1981.
A Christmas Treat. London: Hodder & Stoughton, 1982.
The Rescue. London: Hodder & Stoughton, 1983.
Tales for Telling: Irish Folk and Fairy Stories. London: Pavilion Books, 1986.

Poetry:
On the Bone. London: Greville Press, 1989.

Contents

Introduction

Language is my tool, I want words to breathe on the page, but feeling is my agenda.
  —Edna O'Brien, 1992

"Who's Afraid of Edna O'Brien?" asks an early interviewer in *Conversations with Edna O'Brien*. When the question was posed in 1967, O'Brien had written six novels. With over fifty years of published novels, biographies, plays, telecasts, short stories, and more, it is hard not to be awed by her accomplishments. An acclaimed and controversial Irish writer, O'Brien saw her early works, beginning with *The Country Girls* in 1960, banned and burned in Ireland, but often read in secret. Before she was famous, she was infamous. Her contemporary work continues to spark debates on the rigors and challenges of Catholic conservatism and the struggle for women to make a place for themselves in the world without anxiety and guilt. The raw nerve of emotion at the heart of her lyrical prose provokes readers, challenges politicians, and proves difficult for critics to place her.[1]

In these interviews, O'Brien finds her own critical voice and moves interviewers away from a focus on her life as the once infamous Edna toward a focus on her works. Parallels between Edna O'Brien and her literary muse and mentor, James Joyce, are often cited in interviews such as Philip Roth's description of *The Country Girls* as "rural 'Dubliners'" (1984). While Joyce is the centerpiece of O'Brien's literary pantheon, allusions to writers such as Shakespeare, Chekhov, Beckett, and Woolf become a medium for her critical voice. In conversations with contemporary writers Philip Roth and Glenn Patterson, O'Brien reveals a sense of herself as a contemporary writer. The final interview included here, with BBC personality William Crawley at Queen's University Belfast, is a synthesis of her acceptance and fame as an Irish writer and an Irish woman, and an affirmation of her literary authority.

December 14, 1967, the date of the first interview in this collection, just one day shy of O'Brien's thirty-seventh birthday, she is being interviewed at University College Cork—at a teach-in, a sign of the modest social rebellions beginning in an otherwise very conservative Catholic Ireland. She is there because she is emblematic of that nascent rebellion. O'Brien has, by 1967, published five novels, all banned in Ireland. Her message to the students at the teach-in is that "she wishes them, especially the young people of Ireland, to be free from guilt." Like the students at the teach-in, O'Brien's writing challenged and discomfited the Irish establishment by giving voice to women in a society where women were still disempowered. Relatively young as an independent country and having felt less of the direct social impacts of World War I and World War II, Ireland is just beginning to find its way as a modern society. Mother Ireland and Mother Church spoke, for the most part, with the same voice until the 1970s. The special position of the Catholic Church in the Irish Constitution was removed by referendum in 1973 leading to more open debates of women's rights and issues. Some of the social issues that would have concerned the University College Cork students in 1967 had only just found their way to a small segment of Irish society through the advent of the Irish National Television Service in 1962. This then is the milieu for the reception of Edna O'Brien's writing in 1960s Ireland.

Mary Maher's 1967 *Irish Times* interview, "Who's Afraid of Edna O'Brien," suggests something of the attitude toward O'Brien and her writing and is representative even in its title of the tone of many of the early interviews. The title is an allusion to the 1966 film, *Who's Afraid of Virginia Woolf?* based on Edward Albee's play. The comparison is apt. The film, starring Elizabeth Taylor,[2] provoked some of the same reactions for its "scandalous language" spoken by a woman as did Edna O'Brien's early novels. Maher's interview reflects the "what she looks like, what she writes about" paradox, a recurrent theme throughout O'Brien's early interviews: "and she looked perfectly lovely . . . the girl who writes about guilt, sex, scandal, and disheveled lives." In a 2010 interview with William Crawley, O'Brien comments on her irritation with people who have interviewed her hair and her house as emblems of her and thus tagged *her* as superficial: "Sometimes journalists have come to the house, and often women journalists as well, and have, if you like, interviewed one's hair. And one's fireplace. And they have given, if you like, the caption or emblem of superficiality just because one manages to look half okay." This ironic disconnect is present in many of the interviews, the exceptions being interviewers who know her well. Some interviewers are clearly impressed by her appearance and somewhat intimidated by her work. Such interviews are as much about the lovely, scandalous Edna as they are about her formidable literary accomplishments. She is correct in implying that such interviews have had an impact on the critical assessment of her work.

Although her literary reputation is now largely secure, being an attractive woman, particularly in the setting of an interview, was not, for O'Brien, in the late twentieth century and the first decades of the twenty-first, a literary asset.

Though the 1970s begins with the publication of *A Pagan Place*, an experimental narrative written in the second person, there is little discussion about O'Brien's stylistic innovations in the interviews of the 1970s. *A Pagan Place* is the sixth, and last, of O'Brien's novels to be banned in Ireland though its setting and characters remain in the west of Ireland. Similarly, *Night*, a dream soliloquy, another of O'Brien's experiments in narrative style, published in 1972, is not the focus of serious critical discussion until much later. It is Philip Roth who takes the novel into serious critical consideration in the 1980s. Interviews generally follow the arc of O'Brien's critical reception, with fewer of them in the 1970s.

By the 1980s, O'Brien has established a literary reputation apart from her Country Girls. She is interviewed as a writer and her work receives serious critical attention by such interviewers as writers Philip Roth and Shusha Guppy (*Paris Review*). In these interviews, O'Brien creates a parallel narrative of herself and her work. Read through the nearly fifty years covered by the interviews included in this collection, Edna O'Brien is initially identified with her rebellious Country Girls in her early works, and she does not discourage this identification.

In 1986, her Country Girls undergo a transformation from the initial publication in three separate novels (*The Country Girls* [1960], *The Lonely Girl* [1962; republished as *The Girl with Green Eyes*, 1964], and *Girls in Their Married Bliss* [1964]) into a literary incarnation as *The Country Girls Trilogy*. The subjective Country Girls are now a literary object. O'Brien adds an epilogue to the trilogy, though she maintains that she has never been satisfied with it. This publication of *The Country Girls Trilogy* marks a turning point toward a more rigorous critical reception of O'Brien's work. Interviewers and reviewers now engage with her work as literature and with O'Brien as a literary figure. In 1987, she publishes a collection of short stories, *A Fanatic Heart*, with an introduction by Philip Roth. She has, by now, an established international critical reputation, one quite apart from her persona as the infamous *Irish country girl.*

Through the 1980s, some of her literary pantheon, including Joyce, Woolf, and Beckett, become subjects of plays and nonfiction works. This pantheon also crowds her interviews, sometimes set up like icons on an altar, both literally and figuratively. Many interviewers discuss books by these writers open on O'Brien's desk to specific pages and pictures of idolized writers displayed in her study. O'Brien's allusions to other writers effectively create a narrative of herself as writer. In addition to Joyce, Woolf, and Beckett, a small sample of others that recur most frequently in the interviews include Chekhov, Shakespeare, the Brontë sisters, Flaubert, Proust, and Tolstoy. Names of writers are a kind of *leitmotif* in the interviews, just as they, and their characters, become subjects in her work such as Virginia Woolf in her play *Virginia* and her biography of James Joyce. The sheer numbers, in some cases topping over thirty in a single interview, function at times like a Greek chorus, commenting on O'Brien's sense of herself as writer. The writer's pantheon is one of the most consistent features of the interviews since, as O'Brien repeatedly asserts, her literary education is not formal, but rather a consequence of her unmediated and capacious reading. Her references to writers are also a mode of critical discourse functioning as a code, a way not only for her to interpret the interviewer, but for the audience to understand her.

By the 1990s and into the early 2000s, O'Brien's work returns to contemporary Ireland. Her eye for the underlying emotional current of events is as sharp as ever, but the sense of personal identification evident in earlier interviews is gone. In her 1992 interview with *Irish Times* writer Eileen Battersby, O'Brien is neither subject nor object; she speaks directly, for herself, and about her writing process. Battersby notes a "rawness of feeling" in O'Brien's fiction that may make her work more appealing in the U.S. and Britain than Ireland. O'Brien responds that now her writing "is more savage" and that *she* "is more savage." The Battersby interview spends only a brief moment on *The Country Girls*, to discuss O'Brien's representation of female experience. O'Brien suggests that her concerns are different from what they were thirty years ago, that now she focuses on "the universality of the female experience," a clear shift away from *The Country Girls.*

Beginning in the mid 1990s, O'Brien publishes a trilogy of novels about modern Ireland (*House of Splendid Isolation* [1994], *Down by the River* [1996], and *In the Forest* [2002]), writing about individuals tangled in contemporary conflicts. These conflicts are rooted in some of the same fears and repression that forced her Country Girls to flee from Ireland in her earliest works. In each of these novels, O'Brien presents characters whose emotional complexities are so finely rendered that the characters force the reader to sympathize with them even as we may violently disagree with, and ultimately condemn, their actions. In 1990, Edna O'Brien also begins a series of interviews at Long Kesh prison[3] in Northern Ireland to create the character at the center of her 1994 novel, *House of Splendid Isolation.* The protagonists, a "guerilla fighter" from Northern Ireland on the run to the Republic of Ireland and an elderly woman who is taken hostage in her own house, discover that they are both hostages to their own warped history. In the interview with William Crawley at Queen's University Belfast, O'Brien relates some of her experiences during her research for *House of Splendid Isolation.* As she reflects on the Troubles, a period of political unrest and violence in Northern Ireland from the 1970s to the late 1990s, she remembers a story told to her by a Protestant boy meeting a Catholic boy on Christmas Day in the Long Kesh prison infirmary, the first Catholic he had ever met: "'I couldn't believe that,' he said, 'that the guy didn't have two horns.' And he meant that," O'Brien says. "It's these innate beliefs people have." This kind of epiphany informs the conversations between the protagonists in *House of Splendid Isolation.* The venue and the tone of this interview at Queen's University Belfast, a prestigious university in Northern Ireland, with Ireland's most famous woman writer—a woman, a Catholic from the west of Ireland living in London—is a marker of the ways in which Edna O'Brien's writing career so often delineates the social history of Ireland during the last five decades.

Published in 1996, *Down by the River* is based on the historic 1992 "Miss X" case. O'Brien clearly intends to relate the experiences of a child victim of incest, and the intense and often violent reactions to the victim by those opposed to her seeking an abortion. *Down by the River* is marked by its relative absence from conversations with interviewers, often being overshadowed by *House of Splendid Isolation.* The Belfast Agreement in 1998 marking the official end to the Troubles—and that *House of Splendid Isolation* is so close to the emotional core of the Troubles—likely explains the novel's prominence in the interviews.

The 2002 interview "Deep Down in the Woods" with the *Observer* writer Robert McCrum discusses the third novel in the series, *In the Forest.* The novel is a psychological investigation of the person who murders a woman, her child, and a priest in the west of Ireland. Edna O'Brien's fictional treatment of the triple murder, which occurred less than a decade before the publication of the book, stirs considerable controversy. Her response to the question, "What is *In the Forest* about?" suggests that O'Brien is not following a new sensationalist theme, but yet again examining one familiar in her works—the darker recesses of Irish history: "Ostensibly it's about a triple murder in a forest, but I believe that the novelist is the psychic and moral historian of his or her society. So it's about that part of Ireland I happen to know very well. It's about that part of Ireland, and the darkness that still prevails." O'Brien's statement parallels one she made in 1992 when talking to Eileen Battersby, thematically tying the three works together: "I love Ireland and I hate Ireland. It has given me psychic soil, spiritual soil, and physical soil." This period of O'Brien's writing is marked by her absent presence; she is always in the background, but her works now outweigh her infamy.

In these interviews, James Joyce, O'Brien's mentor and muse, is a central figure. Joyce becomes the subject of a biography by O'Brien in 1999. For O'Brien, writing a biography of Joyce is something of a spiritual incarnation. She has been immersed in the life and works of Joyce since she purchased a copy of T. S. Eliot's *Introducing James Joyce* at the age of nineteen. A copy of Joyce lying open on O'Brien's desk is noted by almost every interviewer who interviews O'Brien in her home. And it is a rare interview in which Joyce is not referenced by O'Brien. She not only speaks about Joyce and his work, she often speaks *through* him when she makes a point about her writing, about Ireland, or the role of the writer. In a 1999 interview with Peter Guttridge, "Schooling for Scandal," O'Brien relates the experience of finding in her initial reading of Joyce, "some similarities . . . and that the key for me to write would be to go into my own life and to dig there." It seems something of an understatement for O'Brien who is sometimes seen as Joyce's female literary successor. Philip Roth's interview with O'Brien quotes Frank Tuohy's essay: "[W]hile Joyce, in *Dubliners* and *A Portrait of the Artist as a Young Man*, was the first Irish Catholic to make his experience and surroundings recognizable, 'the world of Nora Barnacle (the former chambermaid who became Joyce's wife) had to wait for the fiction of Edna O'Brien.'"

Writer Glenn Patterson looks back on O'Brien's long writing career, and sees at the core of O'Brien's relationship with Joyce a shared understanding of language as "a moral endeavor in the rightness of language . . . that language is too incendiary to get it wrong." O'Brien responds, "I wonder if it's moral or if it's obsessive. Anything that's creative . . . requires such a truth, such an intent on the part of the doer." Such truth and honesty, for O'Brien, as a woman writer whose work now bridges two centuries, has come at a cost. Gender was for her, "the fourth net."[4] Patterson, commenting on the totality of her work as a writer suggests that "as the writer in all of your works you have gone where the writing has taken you at whatever cost" (2007). Perhaps this is the resolution of her fame and infamy.

Acknowledgments

Edna O'Brien; the *Irish Times*, Eoin Mc Vey; the *Paris Review*, Nicole Rudick; the *New York Times*; the *Toronto Star*; the *Independent*; the *Observer*; BBC, Vicky Mitchell; The Arts Council of Northern Ireland, Glenn Patterson; the *Belfast Telegraph*; Paul Connolly; Queen's University, William Crawley; Ed Victor Ltd. Literary Agency; Houghton Mifflin Harcourt; The Wylie Agency; Blume Academic Library, St. Mary's University; Emory University, MARBL; University College Dublin, Special Collections; Walter Biggins and Anne Stascavage, University Press of Mississippi.

St. Mary's University, Department of English & Communication Studies. Research Associate, Patricia Amalia Sipes.

This book is dedicated to my American, Irish and Academic families.

AHK

Notes

1. This subject is further approached in *Edna O'Brien: The Fourth Net* by Alice Kersnowski (forthcoming).
2. Elizabeth Taylor also starred in *X, Y, and Zee*, the film adaptation of Edna O'Brien's *Zee and Co.*
3. Also known as the Maze prison, this detention center housed both Loyalist and Republican prisoners between 1971 and 2000. Edna O'Brien's interviews with prisoners at Long Kesh prison were highly controversial.
4. *Fourth Net: Edna O'Brien, an Irish Modernist.* The "fourth net" implied here is gender; the nets are a reference to James Joyce's *Portrait of the Artist as a Young* Man: "When the soul of a man is born in this country there are nets flung at it to hold it back from flight. You talk to me of nationality, language, religion. I shall try to fly by those nets."

Chronology

1930	Edna O'Brien born 15 December in Tuamgraney, County Clare, Ireland, to Michael O'Brien and Lena, née Cleary. She is the youngest of four; sisters Patsy and Eileen, and brother John.
1936	O'Brien attends the National School in Scariff.
1938	Daphne du Maurier's popular novel *Rebecca* published. O'Brien recalls her impressions of the novel as pages were secretly circulated among the women in her village.
1941–1946	Edna O'Brien attends boarding school at the Convent of Mercy in Lough Rea, Galway.
1945	End of World War II.
1946–1950	O'Brien moves to Dublin where she works in a pharmacy and studies at a pharmaceutical college. James Joyce becomes her lifelong muse and mentor following her purchase of T. S. Eliot's, *Introducing James Joyce*, a small book containing excerpts of Joyce's major works.
1948	O'Brien begins writing small pieces for the *Irish Press*.
1950	Edna O'Brien is granted her license to practice as a pharmacist. Ernest Gébler, O'Brien's future husband, publishes his most famous novel, *The Voyage of the "Mayflower."*
1952	Edna O'Brien elopes with Czech/Irish writer Ernest Gébler. The marriage will be dissolved in 1964, but during the marriage, O'Brien's literary success is often attributed to her husband, some going so far as to say that he wrote the majority of the works for her. Sasha Gébler, son of Edna O'Brien and Ernest Gébler, born. Sasha Gébler will become an architect.
1954	Carlo Gébler, son of Edna O'Brien and Ernest Gébler, born. Carlo Gébler will become a writer, producer, and director.
1958	O'Brien moves to London where she continues to live.
1958–1959	In the fervor of three weeks around Christmas and the New Year, Edna O'Brien writes *The Country Girls*, for which she is given a £50 advance.
1960	*The Country Girls* published. It is the first of six novels by

O'Brien to be banned in Ireland. Copies of the book are burned by a curate on the grounds of the local church in her home parish. Edna O'Brien's mother relates to her that women even fainted over what she had written. O'Brien is declared by the Minister for Culture and the Archbishop of Dublin as a "smear on Irish womanhood."

1961   31 December, initiation of the Irish National Television Service (Raidió Teilifís Éireann (RTÉ) opens Ireland to the outside world and marks the beginning of a gradual liberalizing process in Irish society.

1962   *The Lonely Girl* (novel), published and subsequently banned in Ireland; reprinted in 1964 as *Girl with Green Eyes*. Edna O'Brien's short story "Come into the Drawing Room, Doris" printed in the *New Yorker*. She will continue to publish in the *New Yorker*, her contributions eventually numbering over forty. In addition to the *New Yorker*, through her career she will also write for *Harper's Bazaar, Redbook, Vogue, Vanity Fair*, the *New York Times*, the *Irish Times*, and other periodicals. *The Country Girls* wins the Kingsley Amis Award for Fiction. *A Cheap Bunch of Nice Flowers*, O'Brien's first play, staged in London in 1962. Published in *Plays of the Year*.

1963   *The Wedding Dress* (television play for *ITV Television Playhouse*) airs and is published in *Mademoiselle* (November). United States President John F. Kennedy pays a formal state visit to Ireland and his ancestral home in June. JFK assassinated 22 November in Dallas, Texas.

1964   *Girl with Green Eyes* (screenplay) adapted by O'Brien from the novel *The Lonely Girl*. *Girls in Their Married Bliss* (novel) published and subsequently banned in Ireland. Edna O'Brien and Ernest Gebler divorce.

1965   *August Is a Wicked Month* (novel) published and subsequently banned in Ireland. Three O'Brien television plays produced: *The Keys of the Café* for *Armchair Theatre, Give My Love to the Pilchards* for *Love Story*, and *A Cheap Bunch of Nice Flowers* for *Festival*.

1966   *Casualties of Peace* (novel) published and subsequently banned in Ireland. *Time Lost and Time Remembered* (screenplay) adapted from short story *I Was Happy Here* (1965).

1967   *Which of These Two Ladies Is He Married To?* (television play) airs. Edna O'Brien attends a teach-in at University College Cork. Her reputation as a rebel and a voice for women's sexuality makes her attractive to oppositional student movements. Northern Ireland Civil Rights Association founded and modeled on the civil rights movement in the U.S. Attacks on NICRA demonstrations become an important marker in thirty years of violence and unrest in Northern Ireland known as "The Troubles."

1968   *I Was Happy Here* (screenplay) produced. *Nothing's Ever Over* (television play for *Half Hour Story*) airs. *The Love Object* (short stories) published.

1969   *Three into Two Won't Go* (screenplay adapted by O'Brien from the novel by Andrea Newmann) produced; produced as a play in London in 1984. "The Troubles" take hold of Northern Ireland, spreading to the Republic of Ireland and parts of England with deployment of British Troops to Northern Ireland 14 August.

1970   *A Pagan Place*, Edna O'Brien's sixth novel, published and subsequently banned in Ireland. It is the last of her novels to be banned in Ireland, but not the last to cause controversy there.

1971   *A Pagan Place* wins the *Yorkshire Post* Novel Award. *Zee & Co.* (play) published.

1972   *X, Y, and Zee* (screenplay) adapted from *Zee & Co.* [filmed with Elizabeth Taylor]. *Night* (novel) published. Echoing Joyce's "Penelope," the novel is a dream soliloquy. Bloody Sunday (30 January). Thirteen civil rights marchers are shot in Derry, Northern Ireland.

1973   *A Pagan Place* (play) published. Produced in London in 1972, New Haven Connecticut in 1974. The Fifth Amendment of the Constitution Act, 1972, is signed into law in Ireland (5 January), removing the special position of the Catholic Church.

1974   *A Scandalous Woman* (short stories) published. *The Gathering* (play) produced in Dublin, Ireland.

1975   End of Vietnam War.

1976   *Mother Ireland* (a travelogue with photography by Fergus Bourke) published.

1977   *Johnny, I Hardly Knew You* (novel); published (American ed. published as *I Hardly Knew You* in 1978). *The Gathering* produced at the Manhattan Theatre Club, New York. *Arabian*

	Days (nonfiction) published. Edna O'Brien's mother, Lena, dies. O'Brien discovers a copy of one of her books in which her mother had "blacked out all the offending words."
1978	*Mrs. Reinhardt and Other Stories* (republished in 1979 as *A Rose in the Heart: Love Stories*) and *The Collected Edna O'Brien* (both short stories) published.
1980	*Virginia* (play) based on the life and works of Virginia Woolf. First performed at the Stratford Shakespearean Festival of Canada, later performed in England in 1981 at the Theatre Royal, Haymarket, and first performed in New York in 1985. *The Dazzle* (children's story) published. Edna O'Brien turns fifty and celebrates twenty years of writing. By this point, she has written eight novels, two nonfiction books, three collections of short stories, a children's story, five theatrical plays, numerous television and screenplays, and multiple pieces for news and leisure periodicals.
1981	*James and Nora: A Portrait of a Marriage*, (nonfiction) the first of several explorations of Joyce's life and work.
1984	*A Fanatic Heart* (short stories with a foreword by Philip Roth) published in the U.S. by Farrar, Straus & Giroux, a benchmark recognition of Edna O'Brien as a major literary figure. *Three into Two Won't Go* produced as a play in London.
1985	*The Country Girls* (screenplay) produced. *Flesh and Blood* (play) produced.
1986	"Samuel Beckett at Eighty" (essay). *Tales for Telling* (folktales retold in dialect by O'Brien) published.
1987	*The Country Girls Trilogy*, new edition of *The Country Girls*, *The Lonely Girl*, and *Girls in Their Married Bliss*, published with the addition of an epilogue. The epilogue is controversial; O'Brien later states in an interview that she "was never quite satisfied with it." *Madam Bovary* (play adaptation of Gustave Flaubert's novel) produced at the Palace at Watford.
1988	*The High Road* (novel) published with dedication "To my grandson Jack Raymond Gebler."
1989	*Blood Memory* (play) produced. *On the Bone* (poems) published. Samuel Beckett, whom Edna O'Brien knew personally and cites frequently as a great inspiration for her, dies at eighty-three in Paris.
1990	*Lantern Slides* (short stories) published. *Lantern Slides* wins the

	Los Angeles Times Book Award. Mary Robinson becomes the first female president of Ireland. Early 1990s: Edna O'Brien interviews Dominic McGlinchey and others at Long Kesh prison.
1991	*Girl with Green Eyes* wins the *Premio Grinzane Cavour* (Italy).
1992	*Time and Tide* (novel) published.
1993	*Time and Tide* wins the Writer's Guild Award for Best Fiction.
1994	*House of Splendid Isolation* (novel) published. Edna O'Brien interviews Gerry Adams for the *New York Times* (published 1 February).
1995	*House of Splendid Isolation* wins the European Prize for Literature from the European Association for the Arts.
1995–2007	Ireland sees a boom in the economy known as the Celtic Tiger.
1996	Publication of *Down by the River* (novel), based on the Miss X case, becomes the center of public controversy. Edna O'Brien becomes a member of Aosdána, an organization honoring artists who have made extraordinary contributions to Irish culture. O'Brien is a guest writer at the Kerry International Summer School. O'Brien, along with poet Brendan Kennelly, creates a theatrical piece for a Memorial Day honoring Gus Martin (Augustine Martin), supporter and friend of O'Brien and longtime Professor of Irish Studies at University College Dublin.
1997–1998	Edna O'Brien is a writer in residence teaching at New York University.
1998	The Belfast "Good Friday" Agreement is signed, signaling "the end" of The Troubles. O'Brien and poet Seamus Heaney do public readings in support of the public referendum for the Agreement. Ernest Gebler, Edna O'Brien's ex-husband, dies.
1999	*James Joyce* published. A biography in the *Writer's Lives Series*, it is a project of great importance to O'Brien and the culmination of her continual reading and study of Joyce, her muse and mentor. *Wild Decembers* (novel) published; movie version filmed in County Wicklow 2009. *Our Father* (play) produced at the Almeida Theatre. Edna O'Brien is awarded an honorary doctorate by Queen's University Belfast.
2000	*Love's Lesson* (short stories) published. O'Brien receives the Literary Award of the American Ireland Fund.
2001	O'Brien receives the Irish PEN Lifetime Achievement Award with encomium by poet, Nobel Laureate Seamus Heaney.

2002   *In the Forest* (novel), published. Based on a triple murder, it creates controversy, in part because of the perspective. *Iphigenia*, a re-envisioning of the classic play by Euripides, is staged in Sheffield, England.

2003   *Iphigenia [of] Euripides* (play) published. *Triptych* (play) premiers at San Francisco Magic Theatre. Edna O'Brien is playwright in residence at San Francisco Magic Theatre.

2004   O'Brien receives an honorary doctorate from the University of Limerick.

2006   *The Light of Evening* (novel) published. University College Dublin awards Edna O'Brien the *Ulysses* Medal, announces the Edna O'Brien Prize, and appoints O'Brien adjunct professor.

2009   *Byron in Love* (nonfiction) published. O'Brien receives the Bob Hughes Lifetime Achievement Award in Irish Literature.

2010   *Haunted* (play) published. *In the Forest* is shortlisted for the Irish Book of the Decade (Bord Gáis Energy Book Awards). Celebrations mark the fiftieth anniversary of the publication of *The Country Girls* and Edna O'Brien's eightieth birthday.

2011   *Saints and Sinners* (short stories) published. *Saints and Sinners* wins the Frank O'Connor International Short Story Award. *Haunted* is produced in New York. Dermot Bolger launches the Edna O'Brien Lecture Series at the Scariff Public Library, County Clare.

2012   *Country Girl: A Memoir* published 24 September in the U.K., 30 April 2013 in the U.S.A.

Conversations with Edna O'Brien

Who's Afraid of Edna O'Brien

Mary Maher / 1967

From *The Irish Times*, 14 December 1967: 8. Copyright © *The Irish Times*. Reprinted by permission.

". . . and she looked perfectly lovely in the paper this morning, you know." The voice at the other end of the phone belonged to a local resident and conveyed approval. Hair done, perhaps, and a fresh little pair of gloves: the girl who writes about guilt, sex, perversion, scandal, and disheveled lives arrives trimly groomed in Cork.

She was certainly there. Everyone connected with the U.C.C. "teach-in" had seen her, or sat just behind her, or walked past her in the Aula Maxima, overheard her chatting, watched her eating. Through the entire tumultuous weekend, while excited students tossed ideas around with seasoned speakers, while politicians and academics and industrialists and clergy sipped tea and argued and called for action, no one ever quite lost sight of Edna O'Brien. She was there, faintly tickling the public imagination with her irreproachably discreet presence.

We met in the hotel lounge in a callous morning sunlight. There were twenty people milling about, survivors of the previous night's marathon discussion. We squinted in the glare, sat on thready old sofas, and hoped for coffee.

"It's marvelous, but it's exhausting," Edna began. She has a small, timorous voice someone described once as "Winnie-the-Pooh." "The students now seem to be far more political than they were when I was one, and they all without exception seem to be socialists. It's wonderful."

She said she had only come to the teach-in to learn what had happened in Ireland in the half dozen years since she has lived here and wouldn't speak unless she was pressured. (She was, and she did.) The coffee came and we murmured politely over it. Edna suddenly straightened up and whispered:

3

"The way they *stare*. There's a boy over there who came in a few minutes ago and has looked straight at us without stopping since."

But everyone else was looking too, most with more slyness. They glanced over newspapers and cups, and what they saw was a woman with short reddish hair in a turquoise dress, wearing sensible but attractive shoes and racy black mesh stockings on her slender legs. She wore no make-up. In another five years she will be forty.

Her face is girlish and her eyes are not: they are large, aquamarine and tilted, and gaze upward with an expression that is simultaneously appraising and apologetic. There is a general air of something tentative about her, something that apprehensively awaits the executioner, although it is obvious that she has been interviewed to infinity and her replies are persuasively oracular.

They are also painful, tight, and emotional, in spite of the careful construction: "I don't feel I am a spokeswoman for Irish women, sexual emancipation, or anything else. I am motivated by a combination of heredity, circumstances, environment, talent, hard work, and luck, and I feel, quite honestly, that at a time when we have a dearth of writers, I've written as truthfully as I can about what I understand. If afterwards, someone says, well, she is trying to be the Irish Mary McCarthy, or something similar, it doesn't really concern me."

She talked slowly and with her gravely courteous contempt, of the Irish inclination to substitute "chat" for discussion.

"Even these students who seem so courageous still seem to speak too much in generalities. I would like to see one of them get up and say, 'I am eighteen years old, I do or do not believe in God, the Church, sexual intercourse before marriage. . . this is something I feel severely about. It's quite an ironic thing that my greatest handicap is fear, a deep resident fear of violence, aggression, pain, insanity; and quite in contradiction to this I have no fear at all about what I say or think, and I despise what I call 'perambulatory talk' that goes around and around and never hits straight."

She cannot remember ever fearing to write, but she said abruptly: "I never wrote a line in Ireland. That's significant, isn't it? I wrote *The Country Girls* in the first three weeks after I left Ireland, torn in grief, despair, and anger. I still think it is the truest thing I have written: I mean, true in a literary sense, in form. I wrote it very fluently—like a dream, in fact. That and *Casualties of Peace* are the truest in this way. If I could choose only two of my novels to live, those would be my choice."

But Edna O'Brien's own private preoccupation is with the hunt for honesty, and she does not think any of the other three novels are less truthful. The people who have accused her of sacrificing truth for sensation she dispenses with kindly: "They probably mean that they can't identify as well with the later books."

She was silent briefly, and began again, slightly more strangled. "My books are only a fraction of my own personal torment. The big problem for any artist is other people's advice. The critics who say, you know, you should return to your earlier style, or something—that's all a load of rubbish. *Country Girls* was the least self-conscious thing I wrote. *Casualties of Peace* is the most complex, the hardest for people to read, the deepest and most rewarding thing I have written. That and *August Is a Wicked Month* are the inner screams of a very private person. They were something I had to do, and now in a funny way I am ready to come out in the world again."

She never referred to *The Lonely Girl*, only shook her head at *Girls in Their Married Bliss*: "I don't like it at all, and even after rewriting it I feel it's unsatisfactory. It's a very strident book. I wrote it at a very disturbed time in my life. Some people say they find it very funny, and I'm always delighted."

The book she will publish in the spring, *The Love Object*, sounds if anything more introverted than the previous novels. "It concerns one man and one woman who go into an upstairs room to make a life of their own away from the world. But the woman still wants to go out, and she does—to the shop, to see people, to learn—and in the end her disobedience is punished. At the end of the novel she returns to her room, only with another man, and what she realizes is that a man, if he is profound, is a country to a woman."

She has always treated the veiled or forthright suggestion that her work is sheerly autobiographical with appropriate and reticent disdain. "We invent less in lies and dreams than in truth. The very act of describing something makes it true, emotionally true: I write about what I experience emotionally or actually."

The intense subjectivity of her books is inescapable, though, and when she describes the forces in her own life ("as you grow older if you are at all serious you must go deeper into the conflicts that caused you") she speaks movingly, almost hypnotically.

"I was born in East Clare in a large stone house with trees around it and a field. And even though we were not a mile from the nearest village, I always thought of us as being extremely isolated; and the journey to school and the village seemed threatening. I was always in terror . . . the thing I am bitter about, and the only thing I am bitter about, is that as a child I never had any sense of security.

"But in the national school we were read the most marvelous essays, wonderful descriptions of nature, the frost, the sky, the landscape. The happiest association of childhood is the combination of that literature, whatever it was, and the black winter frost of the countryside.

"I had one brother and two sisters, but in my fictional memory I always think of myself as an only child. I identified very much with my mother and found my father rather awesome; I suppose this is the pattern of most Irish families.

"I went to boarding school in Lough Rea, Galway, a town with a lake outside it. It did two good things for me. It gave me a certain discipline, which I can still revert to and go without food or sleep if necessary. It also taught me that no matter what the circumstances you can always escape through your imagination. Oddly enough, when I was there, I was quite happy, and yet when I was out, I wrote about it as severe and uncomfortable.

"I believe this—that we never know what we truly feel about a person, or a place, until we leave it. I don't think I was capable of knowing whether I really loved my parents, or my husband, until I was separated from them."

"I grew up with a God-the-Father idea that asks too much of any mortal man. I have been married once, unsuccessfully. It's a great tragedy to me personally that the relationship I seem to require isn't humanly possible."

"I think two things were always uppermost in my mind as a child: that God created us and that if we didn't obey him we would go to hell, and that my country was tortured for nine hundred years. We are very self-pitying people, and I loathe self-pity. Our sense of martyrdom and our heaven hell-purgatory complex are outrageous in the broad context of life and humanity. The sort of Irish education I knew equipped you to do a job, but not to face the world with any sense of proportion."

It is one of the things she wishes her own children—two boys, age fourteen and twelve—to absorb. "I want them to read widely of different ideas, not to come to conclusions so much as to have a relaxed view of the world.

"I think it's very important at a young age to have access to someone who acts noble, and I hope they can find that. As a small child I began to see the contradiction in the word 'charity' and its application. I admired the saints and thought the doctrine wholesome; but didn't find many people whom I admired and respected.

"I hope they can have the opportunity to learn, to try ideas in a spirit of excitement when they are students like these students. It would be wonderful to have that period between seventeen and twenty-one again. I didn't have the buoyancy that I think young people should have then. I was working in a chemist shop in Dublin and going to pharmaceutical college, and it was a drab life.

"I tell my sons that they are almost certain to have sexual relations when they are seventeen, eighteen, or nineteen, and that I hope it is generated by love. I don't think promiscuity is sinful, but it does reduce the person, reduce the inclination for love." She is not happy about living in London, either for her sake or her children's.

"It's too chic and unsatisfying. The promiscuity in London now among young people is destructive. One of the sad things about freedom is its abuse. But given its alternatives, I still think the English teenagers are luckier than the Irish teenagers. They don't suffer from the same psyche of guilt, and there is nothing more terrible than guilt—it destroys everything, spirit, courage, humor, love."

They are all qualities Edna places priority on. When she spoke of her characters, Baba and Caitleen, the two sides of the same self, she said, "I admire Baba much more. She has courage and humor, and they are everything. Anything else seems tepid next to them."

In some ways it has been easier to be courageous in the past seven years of success—"I can give my opinion now in Ireland without being penalized. I don't earn a penny here. The price has been public stares and speculation and, most recently, a growing public demand for my opinion." She spoke with some irritation. "I resent being told it is my duty to speak when it is not my duty to speak. It is my duty to write what I want to write, as truthfully as I can. To insist that I should get up and speak about economics and culture is impertinence."

She shied nervously but emphatically away from the idea of returning, remarking that it was more probable that she would move to a Central European country when her children were out of school. "I have more rapport with Hungarian Czechs; they see life more as a whole."

A remark she had made earlier, when we were still in the hesitant skirmish of establishing the conversation, seemed to be more important than it had, "I am deeply coursed in this country—my literary organs—mythology, my religion, however much they may burden me, are Irish. I am nourished by the querulousness of the country; its abrasive quality is my incentive to write. Always when I come back to Ireland I feel a great hunger to start writing again; when people tell me sad stories here, they break my heart more. In a small country, the characters of people, the lives are much more apparent and unprotected. We are very vulnerable people."

Edna O'Brien Talks to David Heycock about Her New Novel, *A Pagan Place*

David Heycock / 1970

From *The Listener*. 7 May 1970: 616–17.

Edna O'Brien: I wanted this time, in *A Pagan Place*, to get into the kingdom of childhood. I wanted to get the minute-to-minute essence of what it is when you're very young, when you're both meticulously aware of everything that's going on around you and totally uncritical. I wrote it in the second person singular because I felt that in every person there are two selves: I suppose they would be called the ego and the alter ego. And then there's almost a kind of negative state where things happen to you and you're not really realizing that they're happening to you. And of course the only place that I could set it is in Ireland where all my association, all my dreams, and all my experience is. There is another thing, which is that I was brought up very much on mythology and on folktales, and on verse, and I wanted, as I always do, to write an extremely nonliterary book.

David Heycock: What do you mean when you use the word "literary"?
O'Brien: I suppose Ronald Firbank was a very literary and mandarin writer and he had the wisdom to recognize it himself. He said of his own work that it was mere thistledown. Well, I'd rather write thistle, to tell you the truth.

Heycock: One of the things you've often said is that when you were growing up in Scariff you always had a dream of a kind of ideal metropolis—something like the dream of the three sisters in Chekhov's play.
O'Brien: Although I found the landscape around Scariff, around my house, rather beautiful, I did feel as a child a very strong emptiness. I felt that there

was—and is—a great melancholy and a great hunger for things in the world—for life, information, for adventure. I had that always—because I made the mistake of thinking that the world outside my own world was composed of people of more profundity. I was to learn otherwise. When I went first to Dublin, I remember, quite early on, thinking: my God, how tawdry a lot of it is, how long the Sunday afternoons are. And then I went to London and saw my illusions dwindle. I don't know whether to call it a virtue or a flaw, but I have a dreadful inclination to improve myself—not improve myself socially but rather, like a giraffe, to stretch my neck. I did say to somebody the other day that I wanted to write and write and write and stretch myself, until finally I'm like somebody on the rack. Somebody has said that Kafka's novel *The Castle* is the record of a soul in search of paradise. And I would say that a lot of my discontent is to do with wanting the impossible.

Heycock: Did you feel this when you were a child?

O'Brien: I did. But the thing about being a child is that you don't really evaluate it until you have gone from it. When I think of childhood, I think of endless hours of being out in fields doing nothing, no purpose, moving from one stone to another stone, and then going over to touch the bark of a tree, finding out if it was smooth and then thinking: if I can get from there to there while I'm counting twenty, then something nice will happen. You know, that incredible mixture of sort of fancifulness and idleness—daft. But as soon as I began to grow up, I remember the New Look came in, and one saw photographs of elegant ladies in Dior dresses—just after the war—and I remember consciously saying to myself: "Even if I had the New Look, even if I had one of these attires, what difference would it make to me, in my two lives—my inner life and my everyday life, my thoughts and my behavior?"

Heycock: Do you think solitude is an intrinsic aspect of childhood?

O'Brien: I think it's an intrinsic aspect of everything. Children tend to experience it more because they experience everything more. And of course they do spend much more time doing nothing, so they're more aware of their solitude. But I don't think it's felt worse because the mistake—and it's a rather lovely mistake—every child makes is to suppose that once he or she is an adult everything will take a magical twist. When I was a child, I thought that by the time I was twenty-four my life would have a harmony, that I would be able to govern it whereas when I was young it was governed by other people. And then when you become conscious, the first onset of sadness and wisdom and maybe irony is the day you know that, ruling out earthquake, war, and great political hazards, your life is up to you. And that's a bit of a prod.

Heycock: What did you read as a child?
O'Brien: I read very little because there were practically no books. There were three circulating in the village, *Gone with the Wind* and *Rebecca* and *How Green Was My Valley.* There was such demand for these books that there were loose pages torn out and given from one person to another. I wasn't eligible for any of these because I was the youngest in this family and the youngest child is always, you know, in the wings. But I did read odd pages of them and it was so funny to read odd pages and then myself to fabricate. It interests me very much how things you read as a child shape the events of your later life. Because of *Rebecca*, getting the patchwork of the stories from my sisters and from other people, and knowing it was about a man who married a woman, and whose first wife had been very beautiful, I actually did come to marry a man who had been married, and his first wife was "very beautiful." It sounds a bit silly, but I am convinced the story of *Rebecca* did really influence me very strongly in that. There was another book I identified with completely. My brother won a copy of *Lorna Doone.* And I literally used to try and look like Lorna Doone and I longed to have this great clan of brothers who would sweep off in the night and shoot deer. But I read little because there was no library. There still isn't.

Heycock: Was there ever a moment when you came across one writer and said to yourself: this person expresses all the things that I've felt?
O'Brien: The first book I felt that about I bought for 4d. on the quays in Dublin. The book was *Introducing James Joyce* by T. S. Eliot. It had extracts from all his works and that was the first time I ever read a writer who seemed not to be a writer, who seemed to present life. All these Rebeccas—they were fabrications about fictional people. The first of the Joyce extracts was the Christmas dinner scene from *Portrait of the Artist*, and then there was a story about a girl, Evelyn, who wanted to run away from home. They could have been my experience. When I came to read him, his writing was not like writing, it had life on the page. Life, breath. Then, much later on, when I read Chekhov, it seemed to me that it would be very hard to read anything and not always, and inevitably, compare it with Chekhov and think how lacking or half-lacking it was. I would say he is the writer that I pay homage to, although now I am fastened to Samuel Beckett's works.

Heycock: How important was the Church?

O'Brien: It was obviously much more important than I realized then. I regarded the chapel itself as someplace beautiful. And I did, to tell you the truth, think of the church as being a bit like a theater, although I didn't admit that to myself—you know, there was the priest off up there on a platform and the bell ringing for the offertory and sermons. At the same time I found confession very frightening and I used to sort of rhyme off these sins: I'd cursed, I'd told lies, I'd had bad thoughts. The priest might ask you what was the nature of the bad thoughts, and the bad thoughts were always to do with tickling and kissing. I never had a boy when I was young—I mean I never even had a crush on a boy, I think because I was too withdrawn, and because I thought it was a sin. I was extremely religious: I got out of bed maybe ten or twenty times in the middle of the night to pray, to say little quick prayers and kneel on the cold floor. On Mondays I wouldn't eat bread, and on Tuesdays I wouldn't eat jam, and on Wednesday I wouldn't eat something else I liked—all for the cause of devotedness. I could not now consciously say I believe in God the Father Almighty, Creator of Heaven and Earth—whatever the way it goes: I couldn't say it because I question every word. At the same time all my images, everything that I have a pull towards has some origin in the Church. I was very conscious of, oh God, the souls in Purgatory and the souls in Hell and the fear of Heaven. I used to lie in my bed as a very young child. We were taught what, on the Day of Judgment, God would say to you depending on whether you were going to Hell or Heaven: "Depart from me, O cursed, to everlasting flames," "Come, you blessed of my father, possess of the kingdom that is prepared for you." And because the language was so high-falutin, I remember thinking: I shall get it mixed up and when He tells me my fate I won't remember, his language is so posh, I won't remember which is Heaven and which is Hell, I'll go the wrong route.

Heycock: Did you think about death as a child?

O'Brien: Constantly. Always before I went to sleep I said:

> I pray to God my soul to keep,
> And if I die before I wake
> I pray to God my soul to take.

It was as much part of me as was living, perhaps even more, because the emphasis was on what happened to one after death, because that was for eternity, whereas one's life is a little short space. In another sense Shakespeare says it too: "We are such stuff as dreams are made of and our little life is rounded with sleep." Would that we knew. In my teaching the little life wasn't rounded with a sleep. The second sleep could lead to pretty hot quarters. And much more than the flames, much more terrifying than the tongues of fire, we were taught, and to this day it harrows me, that the great pain of Hell is that of being eternally cut off from the sight of God, of having had a glimpse of God but never repeating it. When somebody says to me as somebody did the other day, "Do you feel you're being punished in your life?" my instinctive answer is: "Yes, because my material life and my working life and so on is very good really, beyond my expectation, but the great love, let us not elevate it, I don't know whether it's for God or man, or what it's for, but the great love that I had some kind of hope and I don't think that could possibly inhabit my life, now."

Our Edna—A Song of S.W.3.

Elgy Gillespie / 1972

From *The Irish Times*, 10 June 1972. Copyright © *The Irish Times*. Reprinted by permission.

Two memories came into my head when I went to see Edna O'Brien. One was of reading *The Country Girls* when I was fifteen and liking Catherine because she was fat and went to dances in frilly blouses, like me. The other was of *August Is a Wicked Month*, which I thought was a souring thing to read, a disemboweling of all female woes too painful to be printed. You feel overpowered by its femininity: all-suffering, all-creating. And so I walked in the leafy square off the King's Road murdering a fast ciggie until she must have wondered what I was doing out there and called me in.

Edna O'Brien does not like being interviewed. She was, she says, once interviewed by a lady she was very nice to, she means really very nice, and this lady was awful about her and accused her of not caring about her children or anything. She, who would do anything for her children, kill for her children. And so now . . . well, would I mind terribly if we didn't talk about her private life, only about her work which mattered most to her? Because she worked so very hard.

No, of course, I said. I was going to write a very cerebral piece about the Irish writer's consciousness, none of your corny old what-does-being-a-woman-mean-stuff at all, oh no! We sat in a blue and white kitchen with a round table and pine cupboards and slate counters to work on, and a plane tree outside the window. A cook's kitchen, well-tended. We drank Indian tea out of blue and white cups, and Edna took her extract of plants recommended by her homeopath for exhaustion, and tasting like Cascara. I shouldn't, she said severely, be smoking. I don't really need it, did I? She felt so much better since giving it up, apart from exhaustion.

I should be imbibing cardamom seeds instead. She thought the plant extract was doing lots of good, because there was so much that was trying in life to cope with. No, she had no one to help her except a part-time secretary three times a week: she did her own cleaning. And she'd done her own decorating, with only one man to help her. Why, she asked, did people ever get decorators in? And every day, letters came, and such letters. Look at this one—"I am a Scotsman born on St. Patrick's Day and I am very drunk and quite apart from the fact that I have just had a quarrel with my wife I would like to write to you to tell you I have just read your books for the second time and liked them very much and I am of course in love with you."

She put the letter down with a what-can-you-do look. And were there, I asked, desperados lurking outside as well as the desperate plans? Oh, yes, because the *Evening Standard* had stupidly printed that she was moving here from Putney a year ago. As for what she was doing here, well . . . she never really thought about what she was doing here. She always assumed she was going to be somewhere else soon, yes, that she was passing through London, but passing through to where? That was the question. "I am an evader; I don't ever confront myself with questions like 'What am I doing here?' and 'What will I do next?' I live so much in my head that it matters not particularly which latitude or longitude I'm in. I am more private here and I have an obsession for privacy. It is necessary for work, the privacy, and that is so important."

She looked pensive (as doubtless, she had looked in front of a hundred thousand interviewers before) and said: "I suppose it is because I am still dismayed by . . . people. I avoid people. Not all the time." (Laughing: irony, bittersweet brand). "Otherwise this heart would not be as battered as it is."

Facts: she is fairly tall, but has narrow shoulders and small bones and so manages to look vulnerable all the same. Her hair is still red and long and curly. She is wearing purple crushed-velvet jeans, a white cheese-cloth smock and a black embroidered jacket. Besides, being in S.W.3. her house has the mirrored Indian cushions, wildly embroidered shawls and nicely exotic junk and Greek goatskins that you would hope for and find in such a London house. You cannot detect County Clare in her voice except when she says "awright, awright" on the telephone, and she is one of the few people who can use four-letter words and make the words sound pretty. From looking around one notices she is reading St Augustine's *City of God* and Sylvia Plath's *Ariel* for a start.

(All right I know this was supposed to be cerebral; I just thought you'd like to know).

She has just finished the staging of her *A Pagan Place*, which is to come on at the Royal Court this autumn; she is to act the part of a schoolteacher who goes mad and flings her clothes off in the classroom. ("I think life is a series of undressings," she adds afterwards, "until you get past all the masks and discover the masks were the person.")

"I would like to tell all the people who tell me I am a sexy woman that I work hard; I would like to take an advertisement out saying 'I have a dull life.' With the odd peak, the odd altitude, thank God. I work in the daytime before the . . . junk . . . of the day piles up on me. But every day there is cleaning and cooking which I love (I am very domesticated, I make my own bread) and at least three things to cope with, like you and tonight this publisher, and then there are dentists and doctors and homeopaths and . . . I sometimes say I have the life of a movie actress without any of the assets."

(More facts: she came to Dublin from Clare when she seventeen, worked in a chemist's shop in Cabra and did freelance work for the press, married Ernest Gebler when she was twenty and lived in Wicklow, came to London in her twenties and lived in a riverside house in Putney. Her two sons are at a coeducational boarding school, they are eighteen and sixteen and, she says, "not ill at ease with themselves, full of curiosity and searching. Like great actors they know how to find their spot. What is it that Emerson says? 'The hero is he that is immovably centered'").

And what of religion? "A man asked me recently, 'Edna, do you believe in God?' A serious man, this was. And I found I was about to rediscover that I wanted to rebelieve. All your youth you are going away from yourself, cutting your hair, growing your hair. You come back a long route."

It happened (the play version of *A Pagan Place*) she says, when she was feeling very barren because she wasn't writing and was worried that perhaps she would never write again. And then, suddenly, her son said it would make a nice play and she started and found it was lovely to write, almost wrote itself. It was work, but lovely work, "It's when you have to, you know, scratch, that it becomes terrible."

At the moment she is finishing the proofs of her new novel *Night* which is a half-apocalyptic book; she quotes a piece about gravestones and milestones and tombstones. "It is a hallucinatory novel." And she is writing a series for Peter Brook which is about a woman who is looking for a flat. *Night* is, she thinks, her ninth book, including the collections of short stories and the filmscript for *Zee and Co.*, a film about which she can only say she is very vexed.

"When you are writing your ninth book, it is a lonely, delving occupation.

And it has so little to do with the [a biting note creeps into the voice] literary world which is, I think, malicious and repetitive." What does she feel about her first book now?

"When I read *The Country Girls* for R.T.E., I came to see it again and it was valid. It is all right like a little bird-note, it's true. I even [note of wonder] cried. I came to write it when I was spending my first winter in London and I was disconsolate and did not understand these locked-up people. Perhaps now I am one of these locked-up people." She wrote it very quickly; *Night* took a year and a half.

She waves at the kitchen, "See, I've come back to slate and wood and a tree outside like the kitchen of my childhood." She has been reading Proust, she says, and finds (this she says very slowly to give me time to take it all down) that our needs, our feelings, and our loves and our half loves are formed in our youth and that as adults we are retapping them in our relationships with men and women. They emerge again. It is, she says, a good idea to go back where we started, to where we first lied, first were frightened, first were guilty and cure them by forgiving your little self; because it is a good idea for people to like themselves; not, she means, self-aggrandizement.

Is that why, I ask, she writes? To try to cure herself? "Oh, I really think now that it is like breathing to me. In the old days I use to say to find myself, to take my revenge or what have you. But I write because I write: a rose is a rose." It is a struggle to face the self like all dance and prayer and lovemaking.

And religion? She is on record as saying, trouble will not cease in Ireland until religion is taken from schooling. "I think religion should not be for education, but for religion's sake. Not that I have any great love of the Catholic Church. I think I love ceremony and litany in my religion. The ritual I found in the dancing of the dervishes; I love movement and I love particularly slow, measured movement." She asked me did I know of a nice service, not just a going-to-Mass-on-Sundays service? Not the Orthodox St. Sophia's; she got vertigo there.

"I was steeped in the Catholic religion and it was steeped in me. But anything that distorts the imagination. . . ." She does not care about being banned; it meant nothing to her, she says.

And politics, "I really think that the I.R.A. have brought Stormont down and they have brought the attention of the world. They have to make huge sacrifices in their lives. And I mean, I would never do that, I could not do that: to be cool, to be brave. . . ." Does she have difficulty expressing this point of view to English colleagues and neighbors? "Oh yes, huge trouble." She had been arguing recently with Richard Neville of Oz, Ink, Alternative

Voice, etcetera. He had asked her how she could excuse things like the tarring and feathering; the answer was that she didn't. But to judge the I.R.A. by one incident like that was ridiculous.

And so what was she doing and thinking about now? Well, there were the poetry readings at the I.C.A. Nash House (her legs wouldn't stand up when she read, she wished there was a pill which would make them keep standing). "Sometimes I get very black inside myself and curled up, not cozy-curled I mean: it's not a nice place to be, the writing state, it's like being on a scaffold. But it's where you have to be to write from the gut and I will always write from the gut."

All this she talked about, and Jung and liking to touch people and hating mental strife and eyeshadow and how Women's Lib didn't take biology and pregnancy and menstruation into account ("There's no getting around that nugget"). And about the hooligans "whose proceedings enlivened the drab monotony of life in Southwark towards the end of the century" (a quote from a book she liked) and how she liked young people and how lucky she has been in good friends that taught her good things.

She began to read a recent poem "Where were you on Bloody Sunday?" ("In the office in the middle of the night, taking down news heads actually.") She looked at me quizzically, and went on reading. And many more things. She showed me a poem she had written called "Shame" which went

> Oh Jesus
> We are giving birth
> It is featureless
> It hates us
> It eats grubs
> We are thinking of calling it Unwanted.

I forgot entirely about the consciousness of the Irish writer living in England and said I wished I could simply give her space for her to fill whatever she wished.

A little reminder, to quote from her first book which she wrote a long time ago before Country Clare girls writing about lovemaking and women's lib Dublin and tarrings and featherings were ever heard of.

"Oh Lord, who does not exist, you hate women, otherwise you'd have made them different."

Whatever you reply to that will be the reason you like Edna O'Brien or you don't.

Miss O'Brien Recalls Hostile Reception Experienced by Chekhov and O'Casey

Peadar Macgiolla Cearr / 1974

From *The Irish Times*, 11 October 1974: 13. Copyright © *The Irish Times*. Reprinted by permission.

A feeling that this year's Dublin Theatre Festival had been successful for the organizers but not for the writer Miss Edna O'Brien prevailed yesterday morning in the Constitution Room of the Shelbourne Hotel filled for the final press conference of the festival. However, half an hour later, as Miss O'Brien excused herself to take her son to the airport one felt that she would survive the savaging in the reviews of her play at the Abbey.

Miss O'Brien's play, *The Gathering*, was the featured event at yesterday's press conference together with a general review of the two weeks of the festival. She was a little late in arriving and when she did was flanked, almost protectively, by the manager of the Abbey, Mr. John Slemon, and the press officer, Mr. Ronan Wilmot.

Mr. Brendan Smith, director of the festival, announced that his final projection for festival occupancy lay somewhere between 84 percent and 86 percent which would be a record. There would be an overall deficit of something less than £3,000, which was within the limits that had been estimated.

Mr. Smith then turned to the journalists and invited questions, but none was asked. Mr. Slemon took the initiative and said that the Abbey was very pleased with the play. The theater was booked out until the end of the week, and they were hopeful that another play by Miss O'Brien would be presented by the company.

Had Miss O'Brien another play ready for the Abbey?

"Not today," she replied from her seat, between Messrs. Wilmot and Slemon, "but perhaps next year."

"When I wake up today and find that I've displeased the critics, I see the knife and I feel that there must be something interesting, some something that caused this. Chekhov, the writer I admire most, perhaps after Shakespeare, had a bad press, and O'Casey got a rough reception from his audience. Mine is an angry play which tries to get to the gut; I don't want cozy work. I ask questions about the family, about skeletons, about love. These are not easy questions and are bound to hurt some people."

Miss O'Brien added that she would like to see the reaction to *The Gathering* as time passed. The reaction to the play would not, she felt, make her discontinue writing plays in favor of writing more novels. When an idea was to be expressed it could sometimes be done in a novel and sometimes in a play. What she had to say in *The Gathering* involved interaction between characters and could best be achieved on the stage.

Mr. Wilmot, who leaves the Abbey this week to establish his own management organization, intervened saying that in all his experience at the theater he had never seen an audience with so many knives in their pockets.

"There was a species interest," Miss O'Brien interjected. "If I had been a fella and a bit older the play itself would probably have attracted more interest."

She referred to Mr. Wilmot's remarks and said that it was amazing how great a part of a play the audience was. On the night of the preview there had been a much more relaxed audience and there had been much more energy in the theater. "I am a firm believer in being steadfast," she said, "and when nobody will give you an inch, you must take an inch."

She was pleased with her cast, she concluded, and would buy each of them a stiff drink.

Mr. Slemon repeated that the bookings were good and that the play would run as planned until November 15.

Miss O'Brien then excused herself and, again flanked by her Abbey escorts, left the press conference.

Miss Anne Makower, whose presentation of *L'Orfeo* opened to a capacity attendance in Christ Church, was then introduced. Bookings were good for the remainder of the week.

Mr. Smith intervened to comment on remarks in one review of *L'Orfeo* that £5,000 had been made available for another production while a meagre £300 been provided for the opera. "Much of the £5,000 goes in the high rents of the theaters, the wages of staff and other overheads in the commercial theaters," he said, "and these costs simply do not arise in regards to Christ Church."

Questioned about difficulty in getting information on fringe events, Mr. Smith said that, if anything, the fringe theaters were developing a greater sense of independence from the festival. He expressed particular appreciation for the work in these centers where so much could be done, especially in regards to late-night shows, that could not be economically provided within the framework of the festival in the larger theaters.

Referring to the demise of the Irish-language productions, which had been a feature of earlier festivals, Mr. Smith was critical of those who did not support these shows, "especially civil servants and others who are getting extra money in their pockets from their command of Irish."

The director was questioned at length about the relationship between the Abbey and the festival, but refused to be drawn into an open controversy, "It does not add to the joys of a director," he conceded, "when, after the program is printed, a show at the Peacock is withdrawn, but the Abbey have their own troubles." He added that when he first heard of the Molière adaptation, *The Happy Go Likeable Man*, his understanding was that it would open during the festival rather than three weeks before it.

"The Abbey have a view," he said, "that in producing *Ulysses in Nighttown* they were bringing back a show which would be of interest to foreigners visiting the festival." He agreed that in the earlier days there had been a lack of cooperation between the Abbey and the festival but, especially in the past five years, there had been close contact with Mícheál Ó hAodha, on the council, and Tomás Mac Anna, on the selection committee, which had contributed much.

After the repeated criticism of the Abbey, mostly from the journalists, had worn itself out and Mr. Smith had repeatedly refused to be drawn, the press conference concluded with the director announcing that next year's festival will run from September 29 until October 11.

Edna O'Brien, The Art of Fiction No. 82

Shusha Guppy / 1984

First published in *The Paris Review*. Copyright © 2004 by *The Paris Review*, used by permission of The Wylie Agency LLC.

Edna O'Brien resembles one of her own heroines: beautiful in a subtle, wistful way, with reddish-blond hair, green eyes, and a savage sense of humor. She lives alone in an airy, spacious apartment in Little Venice, London, near the Canal. From her balcony, wrought-iron steps lead down to a vast tree-filled park, where O'Brien often can be found strolling during breaks from her work. The following interview took place in her writing room—a large, comfortable study cluttered with books, notebooks, records, and periodicals. The day I was there, the room was warmed by a log fire burning in the fireplace, and even more so by O'Brien's rich, softly accented Irish voice.

INTERVIEWER: You once said that as far back as you can remember you have been a writer. At what point did you actually start writing literature?

EDNA O'BRIEN: When I say I have written from the beginning, I mean that all real writers write from the beginning, that the vocation, the obsession, is already there, and that the obsession derives from an intensity of feeling which normal life cannot accommodate. I started writing snippets when I was eight or nine, but I wrote my first novel when I left Ireland and came to live in London. I had never been outside Ireland and it was November when I arrived in England. I found everything so different, so *alien*. Waterloo Station was full of people who were nameless, faceless. There were wreaths on the Cenotaph for Remembrance Sunday, and I felt bewildered and lost—an outsider. So in a sense *The Country Girls*, which I wrote in those first few weeks after my arrival, was my experience of Ireland and my farewell to it. But something happened to my style which I will tell you about. I had been trying to write short bits, and these were always flowery and over-lyrical.

Shortly after I arrived in London I saw an advertisement for a lecture given by Arthur Mizener [author of a book on F. Scott Fitzgerald, *The Far Side of Paradise*] on Hemingway and Fitzgerald. You must remember that I had no literary education, but a fervid religious one. So I went to the lecture and it was like a thunderbolt—Saul of Tarsus on his horse! Mizener read out the first paragraph of *A Farewell to Arms* and I couldn't believe it—this totally uncluttered, precise, true prose, which was *also* very moving and lyrical. I can say that the two things came together then: my being ready for the revelation and my urgency to write. The novel *wrote itself*, so to speak, in a few weeks. All the time I was writing it I couldn't stop crying, although it is a fairly buoyant, funny book. But it was the separation from Ireland which brought me to the point where I *had* to write, though I had always been in love with literature.

INTERVIEWER: If you had always loved literature, why did you study chemistry at university rather than English?
O'BRIEN: The usual reason, family. My family was radically opposed to anything to do with literature. Although Ireland has produced so many great writers, there is a deep suspicion about writing there. Somehow they know that writing is dangerous, seditious, as if "In the beginning was the Word and the Word was with God and the Word *was* God." I was an obedient little girl—though I hate to admit it now!—and went along with my family's wishes. I worked in a chemist's shop and then studied at the Pharmaceutical College at night.

INTERVIEWER: The protagonist of *The Country Girls* also works in a shop. Is the novel autobiographical?
O'BRIEN: The novel is autobiographical insofar as I was born and bred in the west of Ireland, educated at a convent, and was full of romantic yearnings, coupled with a sense of outrage. But any book that is any good must be, to some extent, autobiographical, because one cannot and should not fabricate emotions; and although style and narrative are crucial, the bulwark, emotion, is what finally matters. With luck, talent, and studiousness, one manages to make a little pearl, or egg, or something . . . But what gives birth to it is what happens inside the soul and the mind, and that has almost always to do with *conflict*. And loss—an innate sense of tragedy.

INTERVIEWER: What Thomas Hardy called "the sadness of things," and Unamuno "*el sentimiento trágico de la vida*"?

O'BRIEN: Precisely. Not just subjective sadness, though you have to experience it in order to know it, but also objective. And the more I read about writers, their letters—say Flaubert's—the more I realize it. Flaubert was in a way like a *woman*. There he was, in Rouen, yearning for the bright lights of Paris and hectic affairs, yet deliberately keeping away from all that, isolating himself, in order to burn and luxuriate in the affliction of his own emotions. So writing, I think, is an interestingly perverse occupation. It is quite sick in the sense of normal human enjoyment of life, because the writer is always *removed*, the way an actor never is. An actor is with the audience, a writer is not with his readers, and by the time the work appears, he or she is again incarcerated in the next book—or in barrenness. So for both men and women writers, writing is an eminently masochistic exercise—though I wonder what Norman Mailer would say to that!

INTERVIEWER: Doesn't the theory of masochism apply to all artists, whatever the art form?
O'BRIEN: To some extent. I was reading van Gogh's letters. My God! I'm surprised he cut off only *one* ear, that he wasn't altogether shredded in pieces! But a woman writer has a double dose of masochism: the masochism of the woman and that of the artist. No way to dodge it or escape from it. Men are better at escaping their psyches and their consciences. But there is a certain dogged strength in realizing that you can make those delirious journeys and come through.

INTERVIEWER: Some don't. There is a high rate of suicide, alcoholism, madness among writers.
O'BRIEN: It is only by the grace of God, and perhaps willpower, that one comes through each time. Many wonderful writers write one or two books and then kill themselves. Sylvia Plath for instance. She was much younger than Virginia Woolf when she committed suicide, but if she had survived that terrible crisis, I feel she would have written better books. I have this theory that Woolf feared that the flame of her talent was extinguished or dwindling because her last book, *Between the Acts*, lacked the soaring genius of the others. When a writer, or an artist, has the feeling that he can't do it anymore, he descends into hell. So you must keep in mind that although it may stop, it can come back. When I was a child in Ireland, a spring would suddenly appear and yield forth buckets of beautiful clear water, then just as suddenly it would dry up. The water-diviners would come with their rods and sometimes another spring would be found. One has to be one's own water-diviner. It is

hard, especially as writers are always anxious, always on the run—from the telephone, from people, from responsibilities, from the distractions of this world. The other thing that can destroy talent is too much grief. Yeats said, "Too much sorrow can make a stone of the heart." I often wonder, if Emily Brontë had lived to be fifty, what kind of books would she have written? Her life was so penalizing—and Charlotte's too—utterly without sex. Emily was thirty when she wrote *Wuthering Heights*. I think the grinding suffering might have killed her talent later. It is not that you have to be happy—that would be asking too much—but if it gets too painful that sense of wonderment, or joy, dies, and with it the generosity so necessary to create.

INTERVIEWER: So the catalyst for your own work was that lecture on Fitzgerald and Hemingway. Before that you said that you read a great deal in Ireland, partly to escape. What sort of books did you read? And which ones influenced you most?

O'BRIEN: Looking back on it, it was not so much escape as nourishment. Of course there is an element of escape as well, that entering temporarily into a different world. But I think literature is food for the soul and the heart. There are books that are pure escapism: thrillers, detective and spy novels, but I can't read them, because they don't *deliver* to me. Whereas from one page of Dostoyevsky I feel renewed, however depressing the subject. The first book I ever *bought*—I've still got it—was called *Introducing James Joyce*, by T. S. Eliot. It contained a short story, a piece from *Portrait of the Artist*, some other pieces, and an introduction by Eliot. I read a scene from *Portrait* which is the Christmas dinner when everything begins pleasantly: a fire, largesse, the blue flame of light on the dark plum pudding, the revelry before the flare-up ensues between people who were for Parnell and those who were against him. Parnell had been dead for a long time, but the Irish, being Irish, persist with history. Reading that book made me realize that I wanted literature for the rest of my life.

INTERVIEWER: And you became a ferocious reader, first of Joyce, then of others. Who else did you read in those early days?

O'BRIEN: I am a slow reader, because I want to savor and recall what I read. The excitement and sense of discovery is not the same as in those days when I would get thoroughly wrapped up in *Vanity Fair* or *War and Peace*. Now I set myself a task of reading one great book each year. Last year I read *Bleak House*, which I think is the greatest English novel—I read a few pages a day.

But one's taste changes so much. I mentioned Scott Fitzgerald, whom I read, oh, so lovingly and thoroughly! I loved *Tender Is the Night* and *The Great Gatsby*, which is a flawless novel. So I can say that he was one of my early influences. But now I know that fundamentally I respond to European literature in all its dark ramifications. I think the Russians are unsurpassable. Of course Joyce did something extraordinary: he threw out the entire heritage of English literature—language, story, structure, everything—and created a new and stupendous work. But for emotional gravity, no one can compare with the Russians. When I first read Chekhov's short stories, before I saw his plays, I knew I had heard the *voice* that I loved most in the whole world. I wrote to my sister, "Read Chekhov—he does not write, he *breathes* life off the page." And he was, and still is, my greatest influence, especially in short-story writing.

INTERVIEWER: Later on, when you tried your hand at drama, did Chekhov come to your rescue there as well?

O'BRIEN: I think so, though it is very dangerous to take Chekhov as a model. His dramatic genius is so mysterious; he does what seems to be the impossible, in that he makes dramatic something that is desultory. And of course it is not desultory—indeed, it is as tightly knit as that Persian carpet. Shakespeare is God. He knows everything and expresses it with such a density of poetry and humor and power that the mind boggles. But then he had *great* themes—*Othello, Hamlet,* the history plays. Chekhov, on the other hand, tells you, or seems to tell you, of a profligate family that is losing an orchard, or some sisters who yearn for Moscow, and inside it is a whole web of life and love and failure. I think that despite his emphasis on wanting to be funny, he was a tragic man. In a letter to his wife, actress Olga Knipper, he says, "It is nine o'clock in the evening, you are going to play act three of my play, and I am as lonely as a coffin!"

INTERVIEWER: The greatness of the Russian classics must be due in part to the vastness and variety of their country, the harshness of climate, and the cruelty and roughness of their society (which hasn't really changed) and which enhances the intensity of the emotions and the extremes of behavior.

O'BRIEN: Certainly. It makes for endurance—those long, savage winters. Also being throttled as they have always been. The more you strangle a man, the deeper he screams. Boris Pasternak put his pain to immortal use in *Dr. Zhivago.*

INTERVIEWER: Did that first book on Joyce send you to read the whole of Joyce?

O'BRIEN: Yes, but I was too young then. Later I read *Ulysses*, and at one point I thought of writing a book on Joyce, *comme tout le monde*! I read a lot of books about Joyce and wrote a monograph. Then I realized that there were already too many books on him and that the best thing you could read about Joyce was Joyce himself.

INTERVIEWER: How do you assess him now, and how is he regarded in Ireland?

O'BRIEN: He is beyond assessment—gigantic. I sometimes read bits of *Finnegans Wake* and feel my brain begin to sizzle. Joyce went mad with genius. When you read *Dubliners* and *Finnegans Wake* you feel that the man underwent a metamorphosis between twenty-five and sixty. H. G. Wells said that *Finnegans Wake* was an immense riddle, and people find it too difficult to read. I have yet to meet anyone who has read and digested the whole of it—except perhaps my friend Richard Ellmann. Joyce killed himself with exertion. He went beyond us into a labyrinth of language, and I don't know whether that was a loss or a gain.

INTERVIEWER: The generation before you in Ireland had an important literary scene: Yeats and Lady Gregory and the Abbey Theatre group, and all the people around them, which ran parallel to London's Bloomsbury group and Eliot's circle. Did you have anything similar in Ireland when you started?

O'BRIEN: Nothing on that level. There was a sort of Irish literary scene but I wasn't part of it. One reason was poverty, another that I didn't have an entrée; I was just a chemistry student in a bed-sit. I heard of people like Sean O'Faolain, Frank O'Connor. Samuel Beckett had left and vowed never to return, Sean O'Casey was in England. But it was good for me not to be part of any scene because it meant that I had to do my apprenticeship alone. Sweet are the uses of adversity, are they not?

INTERVIEWER: What about women writers? You haven't mentioned any as a major influence so far.

O'BRIEN: Every woman novelist has been influenced by the Brontës. *Wuthering Heights* and *Jane Eyre*. The poetry of Emily Dickinson, the early books of Elizabeth Bowen—especially the one she wrote about her home in Ireland, *Bowen's Court*. My admiration for Jane Austen came much later, and I also love the Russian poet Anna Akhmatova. Nowadays there are too many writers, and I think one of the reasons for the deterioration of language and literature in the last forty years has been the spawning of inferior novels. Everybody writes novels—journalists, broadcasters, tv announcers . . . it is a free-for-all! But writing is a vocation, like being a nun or a priest. I work at my writing as an athlete does at his training, taking it very seriously. Whether a novel is autobiographical or not does not matter. What is important is the truth in it and the way that truth is expressed. I think a casual or frivolous attitude is pernicious.

INTERVIEWER: Is there any area of fiction that you find women are better equipped to explore?

O'BRIEN: Yes. Women are better at emotions and the havoc those emotions wreak. But it must be said that Anna Karenina is the most believable heroine. The last scene where she goes to the station and looks down at the rails and thinks of Vronsky's rejection is terrible in its depiction of despair. Women, on the whole, are better at plumbing the depths. A woman artist can produce a perfect gem, as opposed to a huge piece of rock carving a man might produce. It is not a limitation of talent or intelligence, it is just a different way of looking at the world.

INTERVIEWER: So you don't believe in the feminist argument that the differences between men and women are a question of nurture and not of nature; that women look at the world differently because they have been conditioned to do so?

O'BRIEN: Not in the least! I believe that we are fundamentally, biologically, and therefore psychologically different. I am not like any man I have met, ever, and that divide is what both interests me and baffles me. A lot of things have been said by feminists about equality, about liberation, but not all of these things are gospel truth. They are opinions the way my books are opinions, nothing more. Of course I would like women to have a better time but I don't see it happening, and for a very simple and primal reason: people are pretty savage towards each other, be they men or women.

INTERVIEWER: Yet your own success is, to a certain degree, due to the fact that your writing coincided with the rise of the feminist movement, because invariably it portrayed loving, sensitive, good women, being victimized by hard, callous men, and it hit the right note at the right time. Would you agree with that?

O'BRIEN: I would think so. However, I am not the darling of the feminists.

They think I am too preoccupied with old-fashioned themes like love and longing. Though one woman in *Ms.* magazine pointed out that I send bulletins from battlefronts where other women do not go. I think I do. The reason why I resent being lectured at is that my psyche is so weighed down with its own paraphernalia! No man or woman from outside could prescribe to me what to do. I have enough trouble keeping madness at bay.

INTERVIEWER: Your description of small towns and their enclosed communities reminds me of some of America's Southern writers, like Faulkner. Did they influence you?

O'BRIEN: Faulkner is an important writer though an imperfect one. I did go through a stage when I read a lot of Southern writers: Carson McCullers, Eudora Welty, Flannery O'Connor . . . Any small, claustrophobic, ingrown community resembles another. The passion and ignorance in the Deep South of America and the west of Ireland are the same.

INTERVIEWER: This is the opposite of the high society and the aristocratic world of Proust's *Remembrance of Things Past*, which has also been a major source of inspiration to you.

O'BRIEN: Proust's influence on me, along with his genius, was his preoccupation with memory and his obsession with the past. His concentration on even the simplest detail—like one petal of a flower, or the design on a dinner plate—has unique, manic intensity. Also, when I read his biography by George Painter I felt the tenderness of his soul and wished I could have met him as a human being. You see, Joyce and Proust, although very different, broke the old mold by recognizing the importance of the rambling, disjointed nature of what goes on in the head, the interior monologue. I wonder how they would fare now. These are more careless times. Literature is no longer sacred, it is a business. There is an invisible umbilical cord between the writer and his potential reader, and I fear that the time has gone when readers could sink into a book the way they did in the past, for the *pace* of life is fast and frenetic. The world is cynical: the dwelling on emotions, the perfection of style, the intensity of a Flaubert is wasted on modern sensibility. I have a feeling that there is a *dying*, if not a *death*, of great literature. Some blame the television for it. Perhaps. There is hardly any distinction between a writer and a journalist—indeed, most writers *are* journalists. Nothing wrong with journalism any more than with dentistry, but they are worlds apart! Whenever I read the English Sunday papers I notice that the standard of literacy is high—all very clever and hollow—but no dues to literature. They care about their own egos. They synopsize the book, tell the plot. Well, fuck the plot! That is for precocious schoolboys. What matters is the imaginative *truth*, and the perfection and care with which it has been rendered. After all, you don't say of a ballet dancer, "He jumped in the air, then he twirled around, et cetera . . ." You are just *carried away* by his dancing. The nicest readers are—and I know by the letters I receive—young-ish people who are still eager and uncontaminated, who approach a book without hostility. But when I read Anita Brookner's novel *Look at Me*, I feel I am in the grip of a most wonderful, imaginative writer. The same is true of Margaret Atwood. Also, great literature is dying because young people, although they don't talk about it much, feel and fear a holocaust.

INTERVIEWER: What about your own relationship with critics? Do you feel misunderstood and neglected by them, or have they been kind to you? Have you ever been savaged by them?

O'BRIEN: Oh yes! I have been savaged all right! I believe one reviewer lost her job on the *New Statesman* because her review of my book *A Pagan Place* was too personal. She went on and on about my illiterate background. On the whole I have had more serious consideration in the United States than in Britain or Ireland. Perhaps because I am not known there as a "personal-ity"! I do not despair though, for the real test of writing is not in the reading but in the rereading. I am not ashamed of my books being reread. The mis-understanding may be due just to geography, and to race. The Irish and the English are poles apart in thought and disposition.

INTERVIEWER: It may also be due to a certain—and very un-British—*démesure* in your writing; I mean they find you too sentimental.

O'BRIEN: I am glad to say that Dickens was accused of sentimentality and, by God, he lives on!

INTERVIEWER: You were brought up as a devout Catholic and had a con-vent education. At one point you even contemplated becoming a nun. What made you give up religion?

O'BRIEN: I married a divorcé, and that was my first "Fall." Add to that the hounding nature of Irish Catholicism and you can dimly understand. We had a daily admonition which went:

You have but one soul to save
One God to love and serve

One Eternity to prepare for
Death will come soon
Judgement will follow, and then
*Heaven—or Hell—*For Ever!

INTERVIEWER: In your novel *A Pagan Place,* the heroine does become a nun. Was that a vicarious fulfillment of a subconscious wish?

O'BRIEN: Perhaps. I did think of becoming a nun when I was very young, but it went out of my mind later, chased away by sexual desire!

INTERVIEWER: Another interesting aspect of that novel is that it is written in the second-person singular, like a soliloquy. It is somewhat reminiscent of Molly Bloom's soliloquy in *Ulysses;* were you conscious of the influence?

O'BRIEN: I didn't take Molly's as a model. The reason was psychological. As a child you are both your secret self and the "you" that your parents think you are. So the use of the second person was a way of combining the two identities. But I tend not to examine these things too closely—they just happen.

INTERVIEWER: Religion has played such a crucial part in your life and evolution, yet you have not dealt with it on any philosophical or moral level, as have Graham Greene or Georges Bernanos; you haven't made religion the central theme of any of your novels. Why?

O'BRIEN: That is perhaps one of the differences between men and women who go through the same experiences. I flee from my persecutors. I have not confronted religion.

INTERVIEWER: Do you think you ever will?

O'BRIEN: I hope so—when I have got rid of the terror and the anxiety. Or perhaps when I know exactly what I believe or don't believe.

INTERVIEWER: Let's talk about the subjects that are dealt with in your work, its central themes, which are romantic love and Ireland. Some people—and not only feminists!—think that your preoccupation with romance verges at times on the sentimental and the "romantic novel" formula. You quoted Aragon in answer: "Love is your last chance, there is really nothing else to keep you there."

O'BRIEN: Other people have said it too, even the Beatles! Emily Dickinson wrote, "And is there more than love and death, then tell me its name?" But my work is concerned with *loss* as much as with love. Loss is every child's theme because by necessity the child loses its mother and its bearings. And writers, however mature and wise and eminent, are children at heart. So my central theme is loss—loss of love, loss of self, loss of God. I have just finished a play, my third, which is about my family. In it for the first time I have allowed my father, who is always the ogre figure in my work, to weep for the loss of *his* child. Therefore, I might, if the gods are good to me, find that my understanding of love has become richer and stronger than my dread of loss. You see, my own father was what you might call the "archetypal" Irishman—a gambler, drinker, a man totally unequipped to be a husband or a father. And of course that colored my views, distorted them, and made me seek out demons.

INTERVIEWER: Is that why, in nearly all your novels, women are longing to establish a simple, loving, harmonious relationship with men, but are unable to do so?

O'BRIEN: My experience was pretty extreme, so that it is hard for me to imagine harmony, or even affinity, between men and women. I would need to be reborn.

INTERVIEWER: The other central theme of your work is Ireland. It seems to me that you have the same love-hate relationship with Ireland that most exiles have with their native country: on the one hand an incurable nostalgia and longing, and on the other the fact that one cannot go back, because the reasons that made one leave in the first place are still there. There is a constant conflict in the soul.

O'BRIEN: My relationship with Ireland is very complex. I could not live there for a variety of reasons. I felt oppressed and strangulated from an early age. That was partly to do with my parents, who were themselves products and victims of their history and culture. That is to say, alas, they were superstitious, fanatical, engulfing. At the same time they were bursting with talent—I know this from my mother's letters, as she wrote to me almost every day. So I have to thank them for a heritage that includes talent, despair, and permanent fury. When I was a student in Dublin my mother found a book of Sean O'Casey in my suitcase and wanted to *burn* it! *But without reading it!* So they hated literature without knowing it. We know that the effect of our parents is indelible, because we internalize as a child and it remains inside us forever. Even when the parents die, you dream of them as if they were still there. Everything was an occasion for fear, religion was force-fed the way they feed the geese of Strasbourg for pâté! I feel I am a cripple with a craving for wings. So much for the personal aspect. As for the country itself, it is no accident that almost all Irish writers leave the country. You know why? Ireland, as Joyce said, eats her writers the way a sow eats her farrow. He also called it a warren of "prelates and kinechites." Of course there's the beauty of the landscape, the poetry, the fairy tales, the vividness. I have shown my love and my entanglement with the place as much as I have shown my hatred. But they think that I have shown only my hatred.

INTERVIEWER: Is that why they had an auto-da-fé of your first novel in your native village?

O'BRIEN: It was a humble event, as befits a backward place. Two or three people had gone to Limerick and bought *The Country Girls*. The parish priest asked them to hand in the books, which they did, and he burnt them on the grounds of the church. Nevertheless, a lot of people read it. My mother was very harsh about it; she thought I was a disgrace. That is the sadness—it takes you half a life to get out of the pits of darkness and stupidity. It fills me with anger, and with pity.

INTERVIEWER: Do you think that after all these years and through your books you have exorcised the demon and can let it rest?

O'BRIEN: I hope not, because one needs one's demons to create.

INTERVIEWER: After that small auto-da-fé, did anything else of that kind happen?

O'BRIEN: They used to ban my books, but now when I go there, people are courteous to my face, though rather slanderous behind my back. Then again, Ireland has changed. There are a lot of young people who are irreligious, or less religious. Ironically, they wouldn't be interested in my early books—they would think them gauche. They are aping English and American mores. If I went to a dance hall in Dublin now I would feel as alien as in a disco in Oklahoma.

INTERVIEWER: You are not a political writer because, as you say, politics are concerned with the social and the external, while your preoccupations are with the inner, psychological life. Nonetheless, considering your emotional involvement with Ireland, how have you kept away from the situation in Northern Ireland—terrorism, the IRA, et cetera . . . ?

O'BRIEN: I have written one long piece on Northern Ireland for the German magazine *Stern*. My feelings about it are so manifold. I think it is mad, a so-called religious war, in this day and age. At the same time, I can't bear the rhetoric of the Unionists; I mean Ireland is *one small* island, and those six counties do not belong to Britain. Equally I abhor terrorism, whoever does it, the IRA, the Arabs, the Israelis. But when I stayed in Northern Ireland to research and write the article, I realized that the Catholics are second-class citizens. They live in terrible slums, in poverty, and know no way of improving their conditions. I have not set a novel in Northern Ireland simply because I do not know enough about it. I dislike cant—you get that from politicians. Writers have to dig deep for experience. I might go and live there for a while, in order to discover and later write about it. But so far I have refrained from bringing the topic into a book merely as a voyeur.

INTERVIEWER: Let's get back to Virginia Woolf . . . Why and when did she become an obsession for you? After all, you are very different as writers and as people.

O'BRIEN: I first read her critical essays, *The Common Reader*, and I saw a woman who loved literature, unlike many critics who just *use* it. The essays are on Hazlitt, Wordsworth, Hardy, everyone. I was overwhelmed first by the generosity of her mind and its perspicacity. Later I read *To the Lighthouse* and my favorite, *Mrs. Dalloway*, which is very spry and sprightly. Then I was asked to write a play about her and I began to read everything she had written—diaries, letters, et cetera . . . I realized that she gave of herself so utterly, so *shamelessly*. Her photographs show her as aloof, which she was in some ways. But in the diaries and letters, she tells *everything*! If she buys a pair of gloves she has to commit it to paper. So I came to know her and to love her.

INTERVIEWER: Some critics pointed to the play's neglect of her intellectual vigor and her bitchiness. Do you think her bitchiness was due to lack of sexual gratification?

O'BRIEN: She did have a bitchy side, but alongside it a childlike need for affection. She called people pet names, waited for her husband to come home, adored her sister Vanessa and wanted her approval. I saw Woolf as a troubled, *needful* creature. Her bitchiness was diminishing, certainly, and she would have been a grander figure without it. I selected those parts of her that chart her dilemma, her march towards suicide. Another writer, say an English homosexual, could write a very waspish, very witty play about her. I hope that mine was valid.

INTERVIEWER: Having been successful at novels and short stories, you tried your hand at drama—plays and screenplays. How did that come about?

O'BRIEN: I was asked to adapt my own novel *A Pagan Place* for the stage and it opened a new vista for me. Then with some experience I tackled Woolf. Now I have written a third play, which for the time being is called *Home Sweet Home*, or *Family Butchers*. I feel drama is more direct, more suitable for expressing passions. Confrontation is the stuff of drama. It happens rather than is described. The play starts in the early morning, the voice of an Irish tenor comes over the gramophone—John McCormack is singing "Bless This House, Oh Lord We Pray," then he's interrupted by a gunshot followed by another gunshot. The lights come on, a man and a woman appear, and you know that this is a play about passion and violence. You go straight for the jugular.

INTERVIEWER: When you start a play, or a novel, or a short story, do you have a basic idea? Or a sentence? Something that triggers off the process of creating the work?

O'BRIEN: I always have the first line. Even with my very first book, *The Country Girls*, I went around with this first sentence in my head long before I sat down to write it.[1]

INTERVIEWER: Once you have started, do you have the whole scheme in your mind or do characters and plot take their own course and lead you, as some novelists say they do? I mean, Balzac was so surprised and moved by Old Goriot's death that he opened his window and shouted, *"Le Père Goriot est mort! Le Père Goriot est mort!"*

O'BRIEN: I know more or less, but I don't discuss it with myself. It is like sleepwalking; I don't know exactly where I am going but I know I will get there. When I am writing, I am so glad to be doing it that whatever form it takes—play, novel, et cetera—I am thankful to the Fates. I keep dozens of pens by me, and exercise books.

INTERVIEWER: When success came and you began to be famous and lionized, did it affect your life, work, and outlook in any way? Is success good for an artist, or does it limit his field of experience?

O'BRIEN: It depends on the degree of success and on the disposition of the artist. It was very nice for me to be published, as I had longed for it. But my

1. "I wakened quickly and sat up in bed abruptly."

success has been rather modest. It hasn't been meteoric. Nor was it financially shattering—just enough to carry me along.

INTERVIEWER: But you have had a great deal of social success: fame, publicity, so on . . .

O'BRIEN: I am not conscious of it. I go to functions more as a duty than for pleasure, and I am always *outside* looking in, not the other way round. But I am grateful to have had enough success not to feel a disaster—it has allayed my hopelessness. Undoubtedly success contributed to the breakup of my marriage. I had married very young. My husband was an attractive father figure—a Professor Higgins. When my book was published and well received, it altered things between us. The break would have come anyway, but my success sped it up. Then began a hard life; but when you are young, you have boundless energy—you run the house, mind the children, *and* write your despair. I don't know if I could do it all now. Looking back I realize that I am one of the luckiest people in the world, since no matter how down I go something brings me back. Is it God's grace or just peasant resilience?

INTERVIEWER: Perhaps it is the creative act of writing. John Updike once said that the minute he puts an unhappiness down on paper, it metamorphoses into a lump of sugar!

O'BRIEN: I think he was simplifying. The original pain that prompted the writing does not lessen, but it is gratifying to give it form and shape.

INTERVIEWER: Did money ever act as a spur? You were very prolific in the sixties, and still are.

O'BRIEN: I have never written anything in order to make money. A story comes to me, is given me, as it were, and I write it. But perhaps the need to earn a living and my need to write coincided. I know that I would still write if tomorrow I was given a huge legacy, and I will always be profligate.

INTERVIEWER: How do you organize your time? Do you write regularly, every day? Philip Roth has said that he writes eight hours a day three hundred and sixty-five days a year. Do you work as compulsively?

O'BRIEN: He is a man, you see. Women have the glorious excuse of having to shop, cook, clean! When I am working, I write in a kind of trance, longhand, in these several copybooks. I meant to tidy up before you came! I write in the morning because one is nearer to the unconscious, the source of inspiration. I never work at night because by then the shackles of the day are around me, what James Stephens (author of *The Crock of Gold*) called "That flat, dull catalogue of dreary things that fasten themselves to my wings," and I don't sit down three hundred and sixty-five days a year because I'm not that kind of writer. I wish I were! Perhaps I don't take myself that seriously. Another reason why I don't write constantly is that I feel I have written all I had wanted to say about love and loss and loneliness and being a victim and all that. I have finished with that territory. And I have not yet embraced another one. It may be that I'm going towards it—I hope and pray that this is the case.

INTERVIEWER: When you are writing, are you disciplined? Do you keep regular hours, turn down invitations, and hibernate?

O'BRIEN: Yes, but discipline doesn't come into it. It is what one has to do. The impulse is stronger than anything. I don't like too much social life anyway. It is gossip and bad white wine. It's a waste. Writing is like carrying a fetus. I get up in the morning, have a cup of tea, and come into this room to work. I never go out to lunch, never, but I stop around one or two and spend the rest of the afternoon attending to mundane things. In the evening I might read or go out to a play or a film, or see my sons. Did I tell you that I spend a lot of time moping? Did Philip Roth say that he moped?

INTERVIEWER: Don't you feel restless and lonely if you have worked all day and have to spend the evening alone?

O'BRIEN: Less lonely than if I were bored at a dinner party. If I get restless I might ring up one of a handful of friends who are close enough to come to the rescue. Rilke said, "Loneliness is a very good practice for eternity." Loneliness is not intolerable—depression is.

INTERVIEWER: Before the film script on Joan of Arc that you are writing now, you wrote another two. One of them, *Zee & Co.*, starring Elizabeth Taylor, was a big-budget, Hollywood film. How did you enjoy that experience?

O'BRIEN: The film world is inhabited by gangsters. I have met many producers and very few of them could I accuse of being sensitive, or interested in writing. They are businesspeople whose material is other people's imagination, and that invariably leads to trouble. People in the clothing industry or the motor business are dealing with merchandise, but the producer's raw material is first and foremost the writer. So I can't say that I had a happy experience. But it is possible; low-budget films like *Gregory's Girl* or *The*

Country Girls do get made. I had a marvelous time with the latter; they didn't have *four* writers all rewriting my script. It restored my faith. I do believe that cinema and the television are the media of the future, more than books, simply because people are too restive. I put as much into a film script as into anything I write—it is, I believe, an art form, and great directors like Bergman, Buñuel, Hitchcock, and Fassbinder have made it so. What happened with *Zee & Co.*—and what happens generally when you get involved with Hollywood—is that you give them the script and then the director or leading actress proceeds to write their own stuff. They are often as capable of writing as I am of brain surgery! So they just disembowel it. And they do it for two reasons: one is ego and the other is ignorance. They know nothing about writing and therefore think they can bring their own *ideas* to it. Now, in the theater when actors want something changed they ask the author.

INTERVIEWER: If someone had time to read only one of your books, which one would you recommend?
O'BRIEN: *A Pagan Place.*

INTERVIEWER: Do you feel that your best book, the one that every writer aspires to, is yet to come?
O'BRIEN: It had better be! I need to develop, to enlarge my spheres of experience.

INTERVIEWER: When you say you are changing your life, do you also mean that the subject matter of your fiction will change with it?
O'BRIEN: I think so. I am giving a lecture in Boston next month about women in literature. I had to come to the forlorn conclusion that all the great heroines have been created by men. I had an anthology of women's writing called *Bold New Women* in which the editor, Barbara Alson, very wisely says that all women writers have written about sex, because sex is their biological life, their environment, and that for a woman a sexual encounter is not just the mechanical thing it can be for a man but—and she uses this wonderful phrase—"a clutch on the universe." I have written quite a lot of love stories; I don't think I want to write those anymore. I even find them hard to read! It doesn't mean that I am not interested in love anymore—that goes on as long as there is breath. I mean I am not going to *write* about it in the same way.

INTERVIEWER: Could it have something to do with age?
O'BRIEN: *Bound* to have something to do with age. The attitude toward

sex changes in two ways. Sexual love becomes deeper and one realizes how fundamental it is and how rich. At the same time, one sees that it is a sort of mutual game and that attraction makes one resort to all sorts of ruses and strategies. To an outsider it is all patent, even laughable. Shakespeare saw through this glorious delusion better than anyone and *As You Like It* is the funniest play about love, yet it is steeped in love.

INTERVIEWER: What about the new cult of chastity? Germaine Greer's new book advocates restraint—a backlash against a decade or so of permissiveness. Have you been influenced by the changing mood?

O'BRIEN: I have always espoused chastity except when one can no longer resist the temptation. I know promiscuity is boring, much more than fish and chips, which is comforting.

INTERVIEWER: Do you find sex scenes difficult to write, considering your puritanical background?

O'BRIEN: Not really. When you are writing you are not conscious of the reader, so that you don't feel embarrassed. I'm sure Joyce had a most heady and wonderful time writing the last fifty pages of *Ulysses*—glorious Molly Bloom. He must have written it in one bout, thinking: I'll show the women of the world that I am omniscient!

INTERVIEWER: What do you think the future has in store for literature? You have been very pessimistic so far. For example, last year nearly three hundred novels were published in France, and few except the ones that won the big prizes were read. Will we go on endlessly writing novels with so few making a mark?

O'BRIEN: As you know the future itself is perilous. But as regards books, there is first the financial aspect of publishing. Already books are very expensive, so that a first novel of quality will have less of a chance of being picked up. Say a new Djuna Barnes, or indeed Nathalie Sarraute, might not get published. If Woolf's *The Waves* were to be published today it would have pitiful sales. Of course, "how-to" books, spy stories, thrillers, and science fiction all sell by the millions. What would be wonderful—what we *need* just now—is some astonishing fairy tale. I read somewhere the other day that the cavemen did not paint what they saw, but what they *wished* they had seen. We need that, in these lonely, lunatic times.

INTERVIEWER: So if we manage to save the planet, is there hope for literature as well?

O'BRIEN: Oh yes! At this very moment, some imagination is spawning something wonderful that might make us tremble. Let's say there will always be literature because the imagination is boundless. We just need to care more for the imagination than for the trivia and the commerce of life. Literature is the next best thing to God. Joyce would disagree. He would say literature *is*, in essence, God.

A Conversation with Edna O'Brien

Philip Roth / 1984

Originally published in the *New York Times Book Review* and currently collected in *Shop Talk: A Writer and His Colleagues and Their Work*. Copyright © 1984, 2001 by Philip Roth, used by permission of The Wylie Agency LLC and Houghton Mifflin Company. All rights reserved.

The Irish writer Edna O'Brien, who has lived in London now for many years, moved recently to a wide boulevard of imposing nineteenth-century facades, a street that in the 1870s, when it was built, was renowned, she tells me, for its mistresses and kept women. The real estate agents have taken to calling this corner of the Maida Vale district "the Belgravia of tomorrow"; at the moment it looks a little like a builder's yard because of all the renovation going on.

Miss O'Brien works in a quiet study that looks out to the green lawn of an immense private garden at the rear of her flat, a garden probably many times larger than the farm village in County Clare where she attended mass as a child. There is a desk, a piano, a sofa, a rosy Oriental carpet deeper in color than the faint marbleized pink of the walls and, through the French doors that open onto the garden, enough plane trees to fill a small park. On the mantel of the fireplace there are photographs of the writer's two grown sons from an early marriage—"I live here more or less alone"—and the famous lyrical photograph of the profile of a very young Virginia Woolf, the heroine of Miss O'Brien's new play. On the desk, which is set to look out toward the church steeple at the far end of the garden, there's a volume of J. M. Synge's collected works open to a chapter in *The Aran Islands*; a volume of Flaubert's correspondence lies on the sofa, the pages turned to an exchange with George Sand. While waiting for me to arrive, she has been signing pages of a special edition of 15,000 copies of her selected stories and listening to a record of rousing choruses from Verdi operas in order to help her get through.

Because everything she's wearing for the interview is black, you cannot, of course, miss the white skin, the green eyes and the auburn hair; the coloring is dramatically Irish—as is the mellifluous fluency.

Philip Roth: In *Malone Dies*, your compatriot Samuel Beckett writes: "Let us say before I go any further, that I forgive nobody. I wish them all an atrocious life in the fires of icy hell and in the execrable generations to come." This quotation stands as the epigraph of *Mother Ireland*, a memoir you published in 1976. Did you mean to suggest by this epigraph that your own writing about Ireland isn't wholly uncontaminated by such sentiments? Frankly, I don't feel such harshness in your work.
Edna O'Brien: I picked the epigraph because I am, or was, especially at that time, unforgiving about lots of things in my life and I picked somebody who said it more eloquently and more ferociously than I could say it.

Roth: The fact is that your fiction argues *against* your unforgivingness.
O'Brien: To some extent it does but that is because I am a creature of conflicts. When I vituperate, I subsequently feel I should appease. That happens throughout my life. I am not a natural out-and-out hater any more than I am a natural, or thorough, out-and-out lover, which means I am often rather at odds with myself and others!

Roth: Who is the most unforgiven creature in your imagination?
O'Brien: Up to the time he died—which was a year ago—it was my father. But through death a metamorphosis happens: within. Since he died I have written a play about him embodying all his traits—his anger, his sexuality, his rapaciousness, etc.—and now I feel differently toward him. I do not want to relive my life with him or be reincarnated as the same daughter but I do forgive him. My mother is a different matter. I loved her, over-loved her, yet she visited a different legacy on me, an all-embracing guilt. I still have a sense of her over my shoulder, judging.

Roth: Here you are, a woman of experience, talking about forgiving your mother and father. Do you think that still worrying those problems has largely to do with your being a writer? If you weren't a writer, if you were a lawyer, if you were a doctor, perhaps you wouldn't be thinking about these people so much.
O'Brien: Absolutely. It's the price of being a writer. One is dogged by the past—pain, sensations, rejections, all of it. I do believe that this clinging to

the past is a zealous, albeit hopeless desire to reinvent it so that one could change it. Doctors, lawyers, and many other stable citizens are not afflicted by a persistent memory. In their way, they might be just as disturbed as you or I, except that they don't know it. They don't delve.

Roth: But not all writers feast on their childhood as much as you have.

O'Brien: I am obsessive, also I am industrious. Besides, the time when you are most alive and most aware is in childhood and one is trying to recapture that heightened awareness.

Roth: From the point of view not of a daughter or of a woman, but of a fiction writer, do you consider yourself fortunate in your origins—having been born in the isolated reaches of Ireland, raised on a lonely farm in the shadow of a violent father and educated by nuns behind the latched gate of a provincial convent? As a writer, how much or how little do you owe to the primitive rural world you often describe in stories about the Ireland of your childhood?

O'Brien: There's no telling, really. If I had grown up on the steppes of Russia, or in Brooklyn—my parents lived there when they were first married—my material would have been different but my apprehension might be just the same. I happened to grow up in a country that was and is breathlessly beautiful so the feeling for nature, for verdure, and for the soil was instilled into me. Secondly, there was no truck with culture or literature so that my longing to write, sprung up of its own accord, was spontaneous. The only books in our house were prayer books, cookery books, and blood-stock reports. I was privy to the world around me, was aware of everyone's little history, the stuff from which stories and novels are made. On the personal level, it was pretty drastic. So all these things combined to make me what I am.

Roth: But are you surprised that you survived the isolated farm and the violent father and the provincial convent without having lost the freedom of mind to be *able* to write?

O'Brien: I am surprised by my own sturdiness—yes; but I do not think that I am unscarred. Such things as driving a car or swimming are quite beyond me. In a lot of ways I feel a cripple. The body was as sacred as a tabernacle and everything a potential occasion of sin. It is funny now, but not that funny—the body contains the life story just as much as the brain. I console myself by thinking that if one part is destroyed another flourishes.

Roth: Was there enough money around when you were growing up?

O'Brien: No—but there had been! My father liked horses and liked leisure. He inherited a great deal of land and a beautiful stone house but he was profligate and the land got given away or squandered in archetypal Irish fashion. Cousins who came home from America brought us clothes and I inherited from my mother a certain childish pleasure in these things. Our greatest excitement was these visits, these gifts of trinkets and things, these signals of an outside, cosmopolitan world, a world I longed to enter.

Roth: I'm struck, particularly in the stories of rural Ireland during the war years, by the vastness and precision of your powers of recall. You seem to remember the shape, texture, color, and dimensions of every object your eye may have landed upon while you were growing up—not to mention the human significance of all you saw, heard, smelled, tasted, and touched. The result is prose like a piece of fine meshwork, a net of perfectly observed sensuous details that enables you to contain all the longing and pain and remorse that surge through the fiction. What I want to ask is how you account for this ability to reconstruct with such passionate exactness an Irish world you haven't fully lived in for decades? How does your memory keep it alive, and why won't this vanished world leave you alone?

O'Brien: At certain times I am sucked back there and the ordinary world and the present time recede. This recollection, or whatever it is, invades me. It is not something that I can summon up, it simply comes and I am the servant of it. My hand does the work and I don't have to think; in fact, were I to think it would stop the flow. It's like a dam in the brain that bursts.

Roth: Do you visit Ireland to help this recall along?

O'Brien: When I visit Ireland, I always secretly hope that something will spark off the hidden world and the hidden stories waiting to be released, but it doesn't happen like that! It happens, as you well know, much more convolutedly, through one's dreams, through chance, and, in my case, through the welter of emotion stimulated by a love affair and its aftermath.

Roth: I wonder if you haven't chosen the way you live—living by yourself— to prevent anything emotionally too powerful from separating you from that past.

O'Brien: I'm sure I have. I rail against my loneliness but it is as dear to me as the thought of unity with a man. I have often said that I would like to divide my life into alternating periods of penance, cavorting, and work, but as you can see that would not strictly fit in with a conventional married life.

Roth: Most American writers I know would be greatly unnerved by the prospect of living away from the country that's their subject and the source of their language and obsessions. Many Eastern European writers I know remain behind the Iron Curtain because the hardships of totalitarianism seem preferable to the dangers, for a writer, of exile. If ever there was a case for a writer staying within earshot of the old neighborhood, it's been provided by two twentieth-century Americans, Faulkner, who settled back in Mississippi after a brief period abroad, and Bellow, who after his wanderings returned to live and teach in Chicago. Now we all know that neither Beckett nor Joyce seemed to want or to need a base in Ireland, once they began experimenting with their Irish endowment—but do *you* ever feel that leaving Ireland as a very young woman and coming to London to make a life has cost you anything as a writer? Isn't there an Ireland other than the Ireland of your youth that might have been turned to your purposes?

O'Brien: To establish oneself in a particular place and to use it as the locale for fiction is both a strength to the writer and a signpost to the reader. But you have to go if you find your roots too threatening, too impinging. Joyce said that Ireland is the sow that eats its farrow—he was referring to their attitude to their writers, they savage them. It is no accident that our two greatest illustrati—himself and Mr. Beckett—left and stayed away, though they never lost their particular Irish consciousness. In my own case, I do not think that I would have written anything if I had stayed. I feel I would have been watched, would have been judged (even more!), and would have lost that priceless commodity called freedom. Writers are always on the run and I was on the run from many things. Yes, I dispossessed myself and I am sure that I lost something, lost the continuity, lost the day-to-day contact with reality. However, compared with Eastern European writers, I have the advantage that I can always go back. For them it must be terrible, the finality of it, the utter banishment, like a soul shut out of heaven.

Roth: Will you go back?

O'Brien: Intermittently. Ireland is very different now, a much more secular land, where, ironically, both the love of literature and the repudiation of literature are on the wane. Ireland is becoming as materialistic and as callow as the rest of the world. Yeats's line—"Romantic Ireland's dead and gone"— has indeed come to fruition.

Roth: In my foreword to your new book, *A Fanatic Heart*, I quote what Frank Tuohy, in an essay about James Joyce, had to say about the two of you: that while Joyce, in *Dubliners* and *A Portrait of the Artist as a Young Man*, was the first Irish Catholic to make his experience and surroundings recognizable, "the world of Nora Barnacle (the former chambermaid who became Joyce's wife) had to wait for the fiction of Edna O'Brien." Can you tell me how important Joyce has been to you? A story of yours like "Tough Men," about the bamboozling of a scheming shopkeeper by an itinerant con man, seems to me right out of some rural "Dubliners," and yet you don't seem to have been challenged by Joyce's linguistic and mythic preoccupations. What has he meant to you, what if anything have you taken or learned from him, and how intimidating is it for an Irish writer to have as precursor this great verbal behemoth who has chewed up everything Irish in sight?

O'Brien: In the constellation of geniuses, he is a blinding light and father of us all. (I exclude Shakespeare because for Shakespeare no human epithet is enough.) When I first read Joyce, it was a little book edited by T. S. Eliot which I bought on the quays in Dublin, secondhand, for fourpence. Before that, I had read very few books and they were mostly gushing and outlandish. I was a pharmaceutical apprentice who dreamed of writing. Now here was "The Dead" and a section of *A Portrait of the Artist as a Young Man* which stunned me not only by the bewitchment of style but because they were so true to life, they *were* life. Then, or rather later, I came to read *Ulysses*, but as a young girl I balked, because it was really too much for me, it was too inaccessible and too masculine, apart from the famous Molly Bloom section. I now think *Ulysses* is the most diverting, brilliant, intricate, and unboring book that I have ever read. I can pick it up at any time, read a few pages, and feel that I have just had a brain transfusion. As for his being intimidating, it doesn't arise—he is simply out of bounds, beyond us all, "the far Azores," as he might call it.

Roth: Let's go back to the world of Nora Barnacle, to how the world looks to the Nora Barnacles, those who remain in Ireland and those who take flight. At the center of virtually all your stories is a woman, generally a woman on her own, battling isolation and loneliness, or seeking love, or recoiling from the surprises of adventuring among men. You write about women without a taint of ideology, or, as far as I can see, any concern with taking a correct position.

O'Brien: The correct position is to write the truth, to write what one feels regardless of any public consideration or any clique. I think an artist never takes a position either through expediency or umbrage. Artists detest and suspect positions because they know that the minute you take a fixed position you are something else, you are a journalist or you are a politician. What I am after is a bit of magic and I do not want to write tracts or to read them. I have depicted women in lonely, desperate, and often humiliated situations, very often the butt of men and almost always searching for an emotional catharsis that does not come. This is my territory and one that I know from hard-earned experience. If you want to know what I regard as the principal crux of female despair, it is this: in the Greek myth of Oedipus and in Freud's exploration of it, the son's desire for his mother is admitted; the infant daughter also desires its mother but it is unthinkable, either in myth, in fantasy, or in fact, that that desire can be consummated.

Roth: Yet you can't be oblivious to the changes in consciousness that have been occasioned by the women's movement.
O'Brien: Yes, certain things have been changed for the better, women are not chattels, they express their right to earn as much as men, to be respected, not to be "The Second Sex," but in the mating area things have not changed. Attraction and sexual love are spurred not by consciousness but by instinct and passion, and in this men and women are radically different. The man still has the greater authority and the greater autonomy. It's biological. The woman's fate is to receive the sperm and to retain it, but the man's is to give it and in the giving he spends himself and then subsequently withdraws. While she is in a sense being fed, he is in the opposite sense being drained, and to resuscitate himself he takes temporary flight. As a result, you get the woman's resentment at being abandoned, however briefly, his guilt at going, and, above all, his innate sense of self-protection in order to re-find himself so as to reaffirm himself. Closeness is therefore always only relative. A man may help with the dishes and so forth, but his commitment is more ambiguous and he has a roving eye.

Roth: Are there no women as promiscuous?
O'Brien: They sometimes are, but it doesn't give them the same sense of achievement. A woman, I dare to say, is capable of a deeper and more lasting love. I would also add that a woman is more afraid of being left. That still stands. Go into any woman's canteen, dress department, hairdresser's, gymnasium, and you will see plenty of desperation and plenty of competition. People utter a lot of slogans but they are only slogans, and what we feel and do is what determines us. Women are no more secure in their emotions

than they ever were. They simply are better at coming to terms with them. The only real security would be to turn away from men, to detach, but that would be a little death—at least, for me it would.

Roth: Why do you write so many love stories? Is it because of the importance of the subject or because, once you grew up and left Ireland and chose the solitary life of a writer, sexual love inevitably became the strongest sphere of experience to which you continued to have access?
O'Brien: First of all, I think love replaced religion for me in my sense of fervor. When I began to look for earthly love (i.e., sex), I felt that I was cutting myself off from God. By taking on the mantle of religion, sex assumed proportions that are rather far-fetched. It became the central thing in my life, the goal. I was very prone to the Heathcliff, Mr. Rochester syndrome and still am. The sexual excitement was to a great extent linked with pain and separation. My sexual life is pivotal to me as I believe it is for everyone else. It takes up a lot of time both in the thinking and the doing, the former often taking pride of place. For me, primarily, it is secretive and contains elements of mystery and plunder. My daily life and my sexual life are not of a whole—they are separated. Part of my Irish heritage!

Roth: What's most difficult about being both a woman and a writer? Do you think there are difficulties you have writing as a woman that I don't have as a man—and do you imagine that there might be difficulties I have that you don't?
O'Brien: I think it is different being a man and a woman, it is very different. I think you as a man have waiting for you in the wings of the world a whole cortege of women—potential wives, mistresses, muses, nurses. Women writers do not have that bonus. The examples are numerous, the Brontë sisters, Jane Austen, Carson McCullers, Flannery O'Connor, Emily Dickinson, Marina Tsvetayeva. I think it was Dashiell Hammett who said he wouldn't want to live with a woman who had more problems than himself. I think the signals men get from me alarm them.

Roth: You will have to find a Leonard Woolf.
O'Brien: I do not want a Leonard Woolf. I want Lord Byron and Leonard Woolf mixed in together.

Roth: But does the job fundamentally come down to the same difficulties then, regardless of gender?

O'Brien: Absolutely. There is no difference at all; you, like me, are trying to make something out of nothing and the anxiety is extreme. Flaubert's description of his room echoing with curses and cries of distress could be any writer's room. Yet I doubt that we would welcome an alternative life, there is something stoical about soldiering on all alone.

Edna O'Brien Takes the High Road

Ken Adachi / 1988

From *Toronto Star*, 26 November 1988. Copyright © *TorStar Syndication Services*. Reprinted by permission.

"Books are always difficult to write," Edna O'Brien, the curator of wild Irish passions, says. "But this last novel was probably more arduous to complete than any other. My nerves were more fractured than normal. It was like carrying a load of bricks on my shoulders."

The High Road is O'Brien's ninth novel but the first in eleven years. She wrote it in fits and starts, in between publishing four collections of short stories, carrying the manuscript from place to place, worrying that the flow of words had dried up, revising constantly.

"I was like Penelope and her tapestry," says O'Brien, who will be in Toronto this Tuesday to read excerpts from the novel in Harbourfront's Brigantine Room. "I kept ripping it apart, until I had some twenty versions to consider. Of course, most writers revise and revise, but not many are as naive as to admit it in print."

Her voice on the telephone from New York is full of her familiar Irish cadences and infectious laughter. And if talking long-distance is certainly not the way one would choose to conduct an interview, at least the memory of a previous face-to-face conversation allows me easily to summon up images of her auburn hair, flashing green eyes, the vivacious woman quick to warm to ideas or lines of inquiry, gentle in refuting certain suppositions.

Why the title? "It works on many levels. I tend to admire people who live dangerously, who show emotions, who are open to experience. The high road in life is one of intensity and drama. It's death, otherwise. But that road can also lead to pain. In a sense, the novel illustrates that great maxim: I suffer, therefore I am alive."

Indeed, the middle-aged narrator, Anna, is a familiar bardic O'Brien figure, the "mendicant from love," carrying to a Spanish resort the sharp and unassuaged memories of an unsatisfactory love affair. There she meets Portia, a past acquaintance from London, who also is in flight from herself and two unhappy marriages. An ex-debutante turned cleaning woman, Portia is now a recluse who grows vegetables and wears dark glasses indoors.

Other women are also victims: the elegant Iris, whose lovers, on departing, tell her: "I hate to do this to you, I hate myself for doing this to you, you don't deserve this"; or Wanda, a divorced mother who complains of her men: "Before you know where you are, you're cooking for them. You're begging your kid to call them daddy (but) just when you think it's all working out, the bastard ups and leaves."

Anna's chief encounter, however, is with Catalina, a young and unconventional chambermaid full of wild passion for life. Anna becomes infatuated with her, invites her for lunch and dinner and evokes the suspicion of her peasant family. In one hike in the hills, they find "not what we sought from men, something other, womanly, primordial." The story, not unexpectedly, ends in blood and tragedy.

Of course, there are touches of infectious humor, even at times of self-parody, especially in the figure of D'Arcy, a painter who talks like James Joyce resurrected. "He's very Irish," O'Brien says, "a mix of the poet and cadger, essentially a decent man who is deeply and always ironic, admitting of emotion and yet scorning it."

The intensity of the novel is pitched high. The Spanish soil teems with vibrant color and objects which assume a portentousness beyond ordinary perception. The Spanish sun both illuminates and blinds. O'Brien invests her sensuous descriptions—of old women in the town chapel, flowers, clothes, jewels, hotel rooms—with meaning and value and conjures up in the reader a response that goes beyond mere physicality.

"That was deliberate," O'Brien says, "and intrinsic to the story. The sheer beauty of the setting is analogous to being in paradise and waiting for the fall. I wanted to set up a contrast between light and dark."

If the effect is finally suffocating, leaving the reader craving for all the artifice to buckle under the strain, then that is the inevitable result of O'Brien's determination to play the game to the end. Indeed, O'Brien is not unlike her narrator, "beautiful, queenly, and even formidable." But she denies—very emphatically—that the novel is in any way autobiographical.

"Of course there are some elements of reality, perhaps bits and pieces from my own past, which provided the germ of the book. I think, for example, every woman, like Anna, wants the love of a woman as much as the love of a man. But my fiction is reality fantasized."

Indeed, the idea for *The High Road* emerged partly from Thomas Mann's *Death in Venice* and perhaps subconsciously from Joyce's short story "The Dead." "They are both about recapturing the impossible," O'Brien says, "about longing for youth. Mann sees in a young boy a reflection of his lost self. This is what Anna, in my book, sees in Catalina."

There is, in O'Brien's novels and stories, always a sense of looking back. Her past is on record, too, in its broad outlines anyway. Its bearing on her emotions and on her writing is direct. She was born in 1932 on a farm in County Clare, in the west of Ireland, and grew up aware of the cramped and narrow world of poverty, hard work, subjugation of women, the weight of religion that crushed people with a sense of sin. She witnessed and experienced physical and emotional cruelty: drunkenness, rage, repression, the loneliness of a painful marriage. It's all in the books.

If she is now Ireland's most famous woman writer (from a country whose most illustrious writers, Joyce, Yeats, Synge, Beckett, O'Casey, and Bernard Shaw, are men), she has paid a hard price. When her first novel, *The Country Girls*, was published in 1960, it was reviled and banned in Ireland for being, among other perceived things, "a smear on Irish womanhood."

O'Brien fought her background, defied her family, battled critics, priests, and censors. "I was slaughtered by the nuns and priests and by the state and made to feel guilty," she recalls. "They would have penalized me if I had remained in Ireland. It wasn't the best auspices for a budding writer. But I was a rebel, I had a lamp of fury inside my soul, just as all my life I have been obsessed with personal freedom."

Writing was her ticket to London. So was her marriage to Ernest Gebler, which produced two sons, Carlo and Sasha, and ended in a messy divorce. "It was James Joyce who said that Ireland eats her writers the way a sow eats her farrow. But I was lucky I was able to go out into the big world, to gain enlightenment."

She also gained the freedom to write the novels and stories of sexual love that account for so large a part of her literary reputation and popularity (among them, *Casualties Of Peace*, *Night*, *August Is A Wicked Month*, *A Scandalous Woman*, *I Hardly Knew You*, *Returning*, and *A Fanatic Heart*). They bristle with unstable energies and articulate a sense of dispossession, the joy and humiliation of love, the bad luck of women fighting loneliness, seeking emotional catharsis or recoiling from unsatisfactory relationships.

She still endorses the spirit, if not the actual letter of the epigraph she used in her 1976 memoir, *Mother Ireland*. It was a quotation from Samuel Beckett's novel *Malone Dies*: "I forgive nobody. I wish them all an atrocious life in the fires of icy hell and in the inexecrable generations to come."

One is awed by those devastating words. She hastens to explain. "No living writer has the magic of Beckett—he's tops!—but perhaps I'm not now inclined to use the second sentence. I have many complex and vacillating feelings about Ireland: an umbilical love coupled with fury over its doctrinaire attitudes. It's the source of my feelings and therefore of my writing."

She goes back for visits and even wrote a travel book, *Vanishing Ireland*, in 1986. "They don't burn my books now, I can walk down the street with a little more ease." The climate has changed. "But would I go back to live? I'll never be out of Ireland in my mind, but I will always be out of it in my body."

Home now, as it has been for more than twenty years, is London, on the edge of Chelsea. She also spends four months a year teaching English literature at New York's City University. "My students are wonderfully receptive and enthusiastic, but teaching is an arduous and exigent task—you can't take it lightly. And if I'm not writing, I feel my existence is floundering. If I'm not writing, I feel starved."

Is there, then, a new novel in the works? "Well, perhaps. I'm thinking of setting it in a Mexican washhouse which I saw last year. I'm going down at Christmas to take another look. Whatever happens, I don't want my next novel to take another eleven years."

Dame Edna

Eileen Battersby / 1992

From *The Irish Times*, 12 September 1992: 29. Copyright © *The Irish Times*. Reprinted by permission.

Although most literary critics would nominate Hemingway as the writer who changed the shape of American prose, there are commentators who would just as easily select him as the writer who demonstrated how the life could become bigger than the work.

After Hemingway, enter Norman Mailer, who is by now more famous for his life than for the work he has produced. The same could be said of the Irish writer Edna O'Brien, who is painfully aware of the way in which her life has often upstaged her fiction.

Since the publication in 1961 of her first novel, *The Country Girls*, O'Brien has been confronted by the outrage of Irish people who resented the Ireland her novels exposed to the outside world. There has also been the endless speculation that all of O'Brien's heroines in novels such as *The Country Girls, Girl with Green Eyes, Night, A Pagan Place*, and *A Scandalous Woman* were modeled on their creator and her own endless quest for love. O'Brien has become a romantic icon: an ethereal, eternal Irish beauty—ageless, timeless, otherworldly, and, above all, a victim.

"Everyone thinks I'm mad, I probably am . . . but I'm not an eccentric. I'm actually very precise, very exact," she says, shrugging with exasperation and amusement. Having lived in London for over thirty years, she knows that observers have decided that she is completely out of touch with Ireland. "But I'm not. I keep myself informed about what is going on there. Of course I know that people say 'the Ireland she wrote about doesn't exist anymore,' but it does, you know," she stresses. "Attitudes don't change, the psyche of a country is not changed by wealth, change is not about getting milking machines." According to her, "the Irish still feed off the human weaknesses and failures of others."

She remembers the outrage and disgust she felt about the handling of the Bishop Casey story. "Those people have their own griefs; the man, the woman, and the child they are not in a happy situation . . . but the country just wanted to expose the fact that a high-ranking priest had got caught. The real story of another man letting a woman down seemed to become lost among the gloating." She comments on the "purience" of it all. "It seems legitimate to dole out smut."

How does she feel about her country now? "I love Ireland and I hate Ireland. I'm glad I'm Irish; it's given me psychic soil, spiritual soil, and physical soil." Europe will have a positive influence on Ireland, "joining up with Europe means an open door, opening a door or a window is always good for either a country or a person."

Two days before the publication of her twelfth novel, *Time and Tide*, O'Brien sits in the book-lined drawing room of her Kensington home and seems nervous. "It's a naked time," she says, conscious that her novel coincides with the announcement of the Booker shortlist. She is a slight, narrow-shouldered woman, taller than one might expect. The famous green eyes are in fact blue/grey, and the rolling rhythmic voice with its Clare accent has a theatrical range.

O'Brien is an emphatic, expansive speaker, often closing her eyes and pushing back against the couch she is sitting on or clenching her fist when reaching for the exact word, "I'm a serious writer, I take my work very seriously . . . I work like a dog, a horse, a slave." While she accepts that her work draws on her own experiences, she describes the process as one of objectifying the material and then making it subjective enough for the reader to be able to identify with it. "I am suspicious of this word 'art'—what does it mean?—I write serious books about real life. Language is my tool, I want words to breathe on the page, but feeling is my agenda."

It is because of the rawness of the feeling she describes that O'Brien's fiction has always been more favorably received in the US than in Britain or Ireland. She has not forgotten that a righteous local priest confiscated copies of *The Country Girls* and burned them in the grounds of the church.

She refers to the peculiarly voyeuristic morality which operates in Ireland. The Irish tend to be less sympathetic than most to the agonies of love. "What I hate is the diminishing and the clichés, I am not a cliché." If she has suffered in her dealings with men, she is certainly not bitter about it. "I like men. In spite of everything, women like men. This is good." However she does make the distinction that whereas a passionate man is a romantic, a passionate woman "is dismissed as an idiot." Most of O'Brien's statements are supported by an impressive line-up of sources, including Aristotle: "as matter desires form so woman desires man."

The career which began with the story of young country girls leaving rural Ireland for the city gradually moved away from an Irish setting and became more intensely centered on the individual experience of the characters involved.

Although O'Brien says she writes about the Irish female experience, she does accept that much of the background detail has been progressively filtered out, she is now focusing on female experience in general. "I am really concerned with the universality of the female experience."

Religion and society are no longer that important, her female characters find themselves in conflict with men. According to her, too much contemporary writing is "merely skimming, it misses out on the darkest, deepest recesses." Real writing, she says, "must crack open the chest bones."

Women who suffer are invariably described as natural victims and it is a word which has been applied so often to O'Brien's characters that she responds by stating: "my heroines are victims; they're not victims. They make bad choices."

According to her, if they were really victims, "after the first emotional blow they'd be sitting alone in darkened rooms eating arrowroot biscuits." On reflection, she is right. Her female characters tend to become secret biscuit eaters. Far from being mild Victorian women crushed by life and the indifference of men, her rebuffed heroines go out looking for love. Nell in *Time and Tide* reacts to the collapse of her marriage by asking a man to sleep with her.

Such a blunt approach may still shock in 1992, yet an earlier O'Brien character, Ellen in *August Is a Wicked Month* published in 1965, adopted similar tactics. O'Brien offended many with her blunt depiction of female sexual frustration, a condition which apparently remains a taboo subject.

While O'Brien in conversation speaks about romantic love, describing life and love as "not an easy journey for a romantic," physical and sexual love are dominant themes in her fiction. She presents longing in urgent, often forcefully violent terms. Much of the earlier lyricism has been edited out, her language has become blunter, harsher, more direct. "It is more savage," she agrees, "I am more savage, I have a savage soul." She pauses and asks, "But what can you do when you're writing about real things such as shock, pity, terror, and escape?"

O'Brien is a reader as much as a writer and says, "Literature is a kind of education." The writers who influenced her through their psychological insights are Flaubert, Chekhov, and Tolstoy. While she says herself that her male characters "have never been as rounded as my females, that's because I'm not a man," she nevertheless agrees that most of the great female characters in fiction have been created by men; "Yes, look at Flaubert, Tolstoy. If Heathcliff is a wonderful romantic creation—that is precisely what he is, a fantasy, a fillet of highly charged female mind, no more. Flaubert in *Madame Bovary* and Tolstoy with *Anna Karenina* created real women by getting inside the female mind, just as Joyce was the first writer to get inside the female body."

The writers of the American South are caught within small, claustrophobic, ingrown communities she understands well, having come from one herself. There was no literature in her family, she studied pharmacy herself. And it was pharmacy, working in a chemist's by day and studying at night, which freed her from the Clare village she grew up in. It has become almost a standard reply in author interviews for the writer to say, "I was always interested in writing," and O'Brien is no exception. "I loved the idea of writing because it suggested to me that life itself could be rendered more deeply and beautifully than normal life as lived."

Of that West of Ireland village between Scarriff and Tuamgraney near Killaloe where she came from, she appears to be neither bitter nor sentimental. But she does speak of the music it gave her; "I love music, I can't sing myself, but I love music and singing, singers."

Where would Edna O'Brien be placed in the canon of international writing? Probably somewhere approaching Colette or Jean Rhys—especially Rhys—in the raw intensity of the experiences she describes. As did Colette, O'Brien wrote her first book with the encouragement of a husband who was for a time something of a Svenghali figure, or as she once described him, "an attractive father figure, something of a Professor Higgins." The marriage produced two sons, but ended soon after the publication of *The Country Girls*. "I was always drawn to men who could dominate me, it makes for pain." Commentators could claim that O'Brien's early fiction is pertinent social documentary.

But all her life, her beauty and strangely earthy *ingenue* quality must have proved a difficult advantage? She seems amused, but it is easy to see how the otherworldly O'Brien could mesmerize a man. "It all depends on a good night's sleep, some days I do have a kind of radiance. But just as easily I look like Lady Macbeth. My face changes a hundred times in the course of a day. There can be a glow or at other times it's like a dud light bulb."

Edna O'Brien could be viewed as either a pioneering feminist or a chronicler of female angst; her women are both dreamers and predator. Her own life has proved a central source, and her material is always concerned with internal life. She does not tell stories or invent fictions, she examines female despair. If she has been a lifelong victim of men, she has also been at the receiving end of some vicious personal and literary criticism. Who is the real Edna O'Brien? Is she an icon or a victim? A celebrity who presents a suitably romantic, strikingly beautiful face of Ireland to the outside world, or is she a wronged Cassandra who exposed repressive Irish intolerance and sexual and moral hypocrisy long before it was acceptable—if it is even acceptable yet—to an unforgiving Ireland which did not want to know and still resents the exposure. Or is she a wounded woman or a detached observer? She is all those things. "I'm a hundred persons," and quoting Hesse's *Steppenwolf*, she says, "Between myself and my other self, there are many selves I have no knowledge of."

Despite what she describes as "a buoyancy," she admits to being "often sad."

When asked to describe the girl who left Clare in the *third* person, O'Brien thinks for a minute and closes her eyes and then begins: "The girl who left Clare brought Clare with her to fill her fiction. And although she was apprenticed to pharmacy, she knew that she would dedicate herself to writing and reading, and that in time that would include rereading. These would be her missions. At the same time she was atavistically hungry for romance, love, and life.

"But the insurmountable difficulties in pursuing both paths made her seem to most people to be both buoyant and somehow illiterate. Her first book, *The Country Girls*, was her ticket, her destiny to life."

O'Brien delivers the short pen-portrait of herself in an almost incantatory style. She asks, "Is that all right?" in that slightly anxious way that she has. Then, when asked to describe—again in the third person—the woman that that girl has become, she again closes her eyes, and recites: "The woman, who lives alone in London now and is a writer, has in her all the elements, all the optimism of the girl who left County Clare, plus her history—her marriage, motherhood, her failures and successes, the love affairs, the problematic love affairs, and the constant daily dilemma of trying to write something good which will make her seem less illiterate and less buoyant," and describe life for the reader.

The Books Interview: A Schooling for Scandal

Peter Guttridge / 1999

From *The Independent*, 12 June 1999. Copyright © *The Independent* 1999. Reprinted by permission of *The Independent*, www.independent.co.uk.

There have already been mutterings in Irish literary circles that Edna O'Brien has had the temerity to write a biography of the Big Man, James Joyce. But even her bitterest critics must admit, however grudgingly, that in just 50,000 words she has caught him, man and writer. O'Brien has been immersed in Joyce for over forty years. She loves language and "the stringing of language," and Joyce's has intoxicated her since, aged nineteen and working in a chemist's shop, she first picked up a copy of T. S. Eliot's introduction to the writer outside Geo Webb's bookshop on the quays in Dublin.

It was a book that changed her life, inspiring her to leave Ireland for London to become a writer. She can quote from memory the section that enflamed her when first glancing through the book. "When I picked up that book I don't know if I'd even heard of James Joyce." She laughs. "He wasn't, so to speak, in the County Clare vernacular. But it was a consummate instruction to me because I saw some similarities. Maybe, I thought, all unhappy families are the same. I also saw that the key for me to write would be to go into my own life and to dig there."

Scarcely a day has gone by since that she has not dipped into Joyce. Love of his writing is not alone, of course, a qualification for writing the biography. But O'Brien—whose seriousness of purpose in her fiction and her life has sometimes been overshadowed by responses to her flame-haired, green-eyed beauty and gossip about her private life—approached the task scrupulously.

"The greatest source were letters, to and from Joyce. And I made use of other books about Joyce, especially Richard Ellmann's biography. And there was the work. It took a year to write but as I've always read Joyce, I like to say it took all my life."

O'Brien once said she would love to write a whole book in Molly Bloom's idiom. "But of course I write screams, while Molly is a holler." She starts the biography with a homage to Joyce's style ("Once upon a time there was a man coming down a road in Dublin and he gave himself the name of Dedalus the sorcerer ... "). "I didn't want to do this whole book like that, though," she says. "I like the variety—the 'plain' writing as well as the somersaults and cartwheels."

The Joyce she presents is a man who suffered much, particularly in his last years—when he was, in her view, a lost man, unable to see, trying to put words down with a crayon, his family breaking up around him.

"When I had read Ellmann, I had concentrated on his halcyon time, on that daring, dauntless Joyce, writing on suitcase lids, impervious to pain, even though he had rejections. But later there was another Joyce, affected by his father's death, the world's rejection of *Finnegans Wake*, and his daughter Lucia going over the brink into madness. I think the gravity of the man, the sadness of the man—a man who had done so much, who ended up stranded and forgotten . . . unable to reach a person he loved beyond words: that's Shakespearean."

Joyce could also be monstrous. "Do writers have to be such monsters in order to create?" she asks. "I believe they do. It is a paradox that while wrestling with language to capture the human condition they become more callous and cut off from the very human traits which they so glisteningly depict." Joyce was shameless when it came to sponging off people: he accepted in the equivalent of almost pounds 1 million from Harriet Shaw Weaver, then would have nothing more to do with her.

"I was a little abashed at the flagrancy with which he took advantage of people in relation to money," O'Brien says. "He was ruthless—but so was Flaubert, so was Tolstoy. . . . Joyce had a terror about money from his earliest experience. He was—as I was and I will never forget it—in the debtors' magazine, *Stubbs Gazette*. So far as I was concerned, all my mother needed after that was for me to write a book!"

There are several odd points of comparison between O'Brien's and Joyce's experiences. "Joyce said that he didn't want to be a literary Jesus Christ," she says. "Well I never wanted to be a literary Mary Magdalene." O'Brien writes that *Ulysses* would have killed Joyce's mother had she not already died. She adds that, for families, "the writer exposes and reinforces their shame in themselves and they cannot forgive it."

"My mother thought *The Country Girls* was the most terrible disgrace," she recalls. "And she said the postmistress said to my father that I should have been kicked naked through the town. There had been no writing in the parish and women writers were unheard of. We talk of Mary Magdalene but it was Jezebel! It was something a young woman would not do. One tries to be understanding, but it cut me."

The outcry *The Country Girls* caused in 1960 has never entirely died down. Although her novels are no longer banned in Ireland, as her first six books were, they can still provoke outrage. The response to her most recent, *Down by the River*, which focused on the anti-abortion movement in Ireland, showed that the bigotry she described still exists. *House of Splendid Isolation*, her 1994 novel about a friendship between an old woman and a young member of the IRA, even earned her a sneering mention in a leader in *The Guardian* as "the Barbara Cartland of long-distance republicanism."

"That is not a standard of criticism for a book, and I'll never forget the person who wrote it. My reply is a version of Gertrude Stein's 'a work of art is a work of art is a work of art.' It has nothing whatsoever to do with whether I'm a Christian Scientist, a Scientologist, or a republican.

"When ugly things are said, diminishing things, for a moment one thinks why expose one's psyche when it's going to be slashed, but it's a very brief moment. You wouldn't be a writer if you didn't have the stamina to keep going. I admire Joyce's total honesty and perseverance—he never stopped. I have that in me from my birth."

She has just completed her latest novel, *Wild Decembers*, to be published in October by Phoenix House, and she will have a play, *Our Fathers*, on at the Almeida by the end of the year. Writing, which she does in longhand, is both a torment and a necessity for her. "It is occasionally pleasurable. . . . But going to it every day and going for a walk and coming back to it and all that old rigmarole is terrifying. Unfortunately, it gets more terrifying. I'm much more exigent now than when I began."

It remains a puzzle that, while she has a worldwide reputation, Ireland is still not won over. "Ireland is a bit hard on me. Perhaps because I don't always live there, I live in London and New York too. For me—Joyce talked about it as well—danger and conflict is at the root of literature, not safety. That means scraping away at the psyche—my own and Ireland's, because I always write about Ireland. They don't like that, I think because they feel it's a woman who has the audacity to do that. But I thank Ireland daily for what it has given me. I sometimes rebuke Ireland, but there are riches."

Deep Down in the Woods

Robert McCrum / 2002

Observer: What is *In the Forest* about?
Edna O'Brien: Ostensibly it's about a triple murder in a forest, but I believe that the novelist is the psychic and moral historian of his or her society. So it's about that part of Ireland I happen to know very well. It's about that part of Ireland, and the darkness that still prevails.

Obs: Was there a specific moment of inspiration, like a news story?
O'Brien: News stories are anathema to fiction. I was researching a previous book and I was brought to the forest, to the spot where this murder happened, where the body of a woman and child were found in a shallow grave. I am not like W. B. Yeats, totally given over to the occult, neither do I dismiss it. I felt, without any shadow of doubt, a trigger which said, "You must tell this story."

Obs: So it was a news story?
O'Brien: The actual event was, but it was not then that I decided to write it. That was much later.

Obs: It's a contemporary story, but your picture of Ireland is quite old-fashioned.
O'Brien: Primitive might be the word. Countries are. You get change in a country, but that doesn't eliminate what already exists. The picture I paint is one of fear.

Obs: How familiar are you with contemporary Ireland?

O'Brien: Very. This makes people annoyed. There is this notion that you have to live in a place, day in, day out. James Joyce was luckier than me, he had more relatives that he could badger. I go there a lot. Like any practicing writer I'm very conscious of what's going on around me. Ireland is what I always write about.

Obs: When did you first know you wanted to be a writer?
O'Brien: Always. The spell and magic and transfiguration that language brings has always obsessed me. I also love story. One of the quarrels I have with contemporary fiction is you don't get a rich story.

Obs: Your debut with *The Country Girls* was sensational. Was that success a good thing or a bad thing?
O'Brien: When *The Country Girls* was published I had only ructions. My family at home in Ireland was shocked. They thought it was a betrayal. They thought I had opened them up to shame. I didn't feel any of the rewards. I can honestly say it in no way spoilt me. I know, without sounding too masochistic, that I must not only write but keep writing, keep on the point of the sword.

Obs: What keeps you "on the point of the sword"?
O'Brien: One has to be, first, disturbed. Second, the state of disturbance that drives one to prose or drama or poetry can get softened by too much celebration. Sometimes I may have railed against my fate, but I have been lucky enough not to have been stopped by either barrenness or by total success. So *The Country Girls* was just the start of a long journey.

Obs: There was a time when your books suffered critical neglect. Was that difficult?
O'Brien: Very difficult. I despise fashion. The only imperative is to do the next book and the next.

Obs: Did you ever doubt yourself?
O'Brien: No, I don't. It's funny, I'm quite insecure in many ways and extremely nervous on this Earth, but I do not doubt what I do.

Obs: Who were the writers that you read as a young girl? Who were the ones who influenced you?
O'Brien: There were none in County Clare. I had read some scripture which

is very beautiful and heard the Gospels, and at school we had fairy tales and heroic tales, not a great deal, I might add. My first [Damascene experience] of literature was by chance one day reading a fragment of James Joyce.

Obs: *Ulysses*?
O'Brien: I wouldn't have been up to *Ulysses* then. It was a little book for fourpence on the quays at Dublin, published by Faber. It was two short stories, a bit of *Portrait*, a bit of *Ulysses*, and a bit of *Finnegans Wake*. It meant so much to me, it was a complete and ultimate education.

Obs: How familiar were you, as a young girl, with the Irish language?
O'Brien: Oh, I learned through Irish. All my life there's a kind of dichotomy: Irish was in the school and English was at home.

Obs: Would you say your work was rooted in the Irish language?
O'Brien: My work is influenced by my religion, by my parents, particularly my mother. She influences me a great deal. But also the place. My books are a part of County Clare, the place is as strong in the books as the characters of the story.

Obs: Do you think that somebody from Clare would recognize it as being Clare?
O'Brien: Oh, they do.

Obs: Do they say it's a caricature?
O'Brien: I think they think it's too revealing.

Obs: So you aren't particular popular at home?
O'Brien: There is more uproar over *In the Forest* than over *The Country Girls*.

Obs: What do you say to people who say you have no right to write the story?
O'Brien: Any writer has the right to write any story. You can tell the "story" in four lines. The tone and nature and intensity of the book is what matters.

Obs: Have any of the people who were part of the original story been in touch with you?
O'Brien: I've had some very barbaric letters, unsigned.

Obs: "Looking up, she saw human faces between tombstones. Joking faces that were laughing and she knew that at that moment she too was turning mad." Do you mean to imply that Ireland is a place that makes you mad?

O'Brien: Tragedy makes people mad, whether it's Ireland or the West Bank. In the two years and three months of writing the book I went to the edge. I had to live with material as dark and as shuddering as this and I had nightmare upon nightmare. So it's not just the Irish are mad, although they probably have quite a good monopoly on it.

Obs: At the very end of the novel you have a line: Magic follows only the few. What did you mean by that?

O'Brien: It's a bit of a mystery to me, that little chapter. I think I meant the magic that story and imagination can, even briefly, create against a bulwark of nightmare, death, and non-resurrection.

Obs: So this book was very painful for you to write?

O'Brien: It was hell.

Obs: What next?

O'Brien: Well, I have just done a free and I suppose extended version of *Iphegenia*. I learn more from the Greeks than from anyone. Well, you learn more from Shakespeare than anyone. Then after that, total radicalization of language from Joyce and the most powerful permeating and permanent stories from the Greeks. I mean, one doesn't need any more. At least I don't.

Obs: If you had to choose between Aeschylus, Shakespeare, and Joyce, who would you choose?

O'Brien: This is a very hard question. Why not have a trinity? If God made a trinity, I'll make a trinity.

Iphigenia

Francine Stock / 2003

From *Front Row*, BBC Radio 4, 7 February 2003. Copyright © "Front Row" BBC Radio 4. Reprinted by permission

We begin with Greek tragedies, specifically the fate of Iphigenia, the daughter of Agamemnon and Clytemnestra. In the play by Euripides, the king is persuaded to sacrifice his daughter so that the goddess Artemis might look favorable upon his forces in the forthcoming assault on the city of Troy. The soldiers are waiting for wind to sail to Troy to reclaim Helen, wife of Menelaus. Iphigenia's death will trigger a further cycle of murder and revenge in the house of Atreus. That's the shadow that hangs over the future in the end of the play, most of *Iphigenia* is concerned with the father's duping of a young girl and her mother for political purposes. The Irish writer Edna O'Brien is the latest to adapt *Iphigenia in Aeoulus*, and when I spoke to her a little earlier she explained the enduring power of Greek tragedy:

Edna O'Brien: The story is as valid and as urgent today as it was when it was written five hundred years before Christ. The story being, as you know, the human drama, the human tension, the human question about the validity of war and why people go to war. Why men go to war. Why they have gone to war down the centuries. Is it for right? Is it for morality to be better or is it for human beings or is it partly to do with their inner sense of conquest?

Francine Stock: Now, you've called this a free adaptation, there are, obviously, many translations of *Iphigenia* already existing; what did you feel you could add?
O'Brien: I removed most of the chorus because the chorus embellish and retell what is going to happen over and over again, and while that might have been wonderful in open air Greek theaters, it is no longer applicable

to now. Second change is Euripides didn't finish the play. It was finished by other hands, and the other hands changed the ending. They softened it to have a deer sacrificed. And it seemed to me, and it will always seem to me, that that softening, and if you like, that total abnegation of everything that had gone on previously in the play and in the drama was suddenly thrown out the window.

Stock: And, as far as the language is concerned, you've made it sound contemporary, but by cutting, of course, some of the chorus sections you have lost some of the perhaps more lyrical and elaborate passages. Do you think that that weakens the play in any way?

O'Brien: I have choruses, I haven't no choruses. I have two women. One is the voice of the appetite for war. The appetite for sacrifice. The appetite for blood. And her opposite is the one who prays that the Goddess—in this case, it could be the God, but it's a Goddess—would avert this slaughter. So it isn't that I have removed the chorus, and I love their lyrical language; but I don't think the stage is the place for long reams of lyrical language. And I'll tell you this, the greatest teacher, let alone genius of this for anyone writing a play, is Shakespeare. Shakespeare knows when to be lyrical and he knows when to cut it.

Stock: It must, nonetheless, be difficult to gauge what type of language is appropriate for something like this because, as you say, you wanted to make it kind of contemporary in some ways so it sounded reasonably colloquial, but occasionally there's a phrase, at one point where you say something about not lumping me in with something else, and I slightly kind of stopped at that and thought, oh?

O'Brien: Yes, that's Clytemnestra. Well, I thought about that word. I thought about it and I decided it was a very organic word so I stayed with it. As regards to the language throughout, I don't sit down and think, "Oh now, I better choose a language that will please this person or that academic or that ordinary theater goer." I chose the language that I had A) a freedom with and B) a confidence in. And that's my imaginative decision.

Stock: Some people spoke of your last novel, *In the Forest*, as though it were Greek tragedy, I mean, is there any connection, do you think?

O'Brien: Oh yes, it was a Greek tragedy. It was a Greek tragedy that happened. Three people are slaughtered in a forest. In "Iphigenia," a girl is also going to be brought to a forest, to the Grove of Artemis, for a slaughter which is given the noble name of sacrifice.

Stock: Was there any sense that after the controversy that surrounded *In the Forest* that you wished to, by returning to one of the classics, avoid anything that might appear to be as contentious?

O'Brien: Oh, not at all. The opposite. The people who attack one or take issue, their reasons are very often quite specious. They are not about "Is something a work of art, is the language, does the language stand up?" They are about prejudice. So I would not let anybody be the decider to tell me what to write or what not to write. It is hard enough anyhow to write, in fact, it's Hell. But my intent and journey with *In the Forest* and *Iphigenia* is to make the journey that I know is very dark that I know, at the same time, is very rich in its human narrative.

Stock: When I read *In the Forest*, I didn't in any way doubt that it was a work of art, and I thought that it was beautifully written, but it did make me uneasy that members of the family had not been happy that you should pursue the story.

O'Brien: Well, you read journalists who said that, but it's not actually true. One person who had been a partner—an estranged partner—of the dead woman made quite a lot of commotion, but no blood relative did, I can assure you of that.

Conversation with Edna O'Brien

Glenn Patterson / 2007

Interview conducted during Art at the Heart Conference, Arts Council of Northern Ireland, Grand Opera Hotel, Belfast, Northern Ireland, 8 November 2007. Copyright © Glenn Patterson. Reprinted with permission.

Glenn Patterson: The way you talk about your writing and the relationship with language calls to mind the writer you have referred to as not just your hero, but your master: Joyce. In fact, you've just written a biography of Joyce for *Penguin Lives*.

O'Brien: Yeah, a brief life. Even though it was brief, that wasn't easy either. I remember once, I was in New York teaching a term at NYU, and I had many books on Joyce. There are a lot of books, as you know, on Joyce. Some are completely unfathomable. They're like written in *Finnegans Wake* language. So Philip Roth comes in to visit me and I'm not looking my best and I'm not feeling my best and all these books I had got including Richard Ellmann's massive and great biography of Joyce. Philip sees all these books along the floor and, to put it mildly, my constrained expression and he gave me a little dig—he's very mischievous—and said, "I bet you think the made-up stuff is easier." And I don't know which is easier. The beautiful poem—why I should say this out of the blue, because it doesn't refer to what we are talking about—of Wallace Stevens that I often think writing or non-writing is; either the act of writing or the waiting for it:

> I do not know which to prefer,
> The beauty of inflection
> Or the beauty of innuendo,
> The blackbird whistling
> Or just after.

And when one finishes a book, as you have just done, as you have told me out there, it's a very lovely, brief feeling. It's a lovely feeling for a very short length of time because the next one has to be done.

Patterson: Just on Joyce for a minute more; it seems to me, listening to you talk and reading the work, that it's not just an aesthetic pursuit, it's almost a moral endeavor in the rightness of language. And I think there's a very public aspect to that—that you feel a moral duty as the writer to get it right—that language is too incendiary, to use the phrase that you use when you talked about your mother, to get it wrong.

O'Brien: I wonder if it's moral or if it's obsessive. Moral, it's true, it's just the word carries in it that a book should be sedate, like a country diary of an Edwardian lady—which, by the way, I wish I could write. I'd be much better if I could write books that were more palatable. It is an impulse, a pulse, a compulsion, and certainly it allows for no rest at all. I noticed Rosalyn in the wings there walking about, and I thought, "Oh my God, how can she do it?" Anything that's creative, whether it's juggling, tightrope walking, writing, acting, or good dentistry, for that matter, requires such a truth and such an intent on the part of the doer. Where it might be called moral, would be in the person's need to make that flawless and having a truth that you can't contradict. But it's not moral in the sense that—to go back to Anne Enright's quote although I don't, I have to confess to everyone here, which is a bit of a disappointment in our hedonist times, I don't think that my books are very sexual at all, so where Anne Enright got this idea was, I imagine, a projection—that morality isn't the business of writing, magic is, and finding that magic: that's the journey.

Patterson: I should say at this stage, because we're going to have to draw to a close quite soon, Anne's review of *The Light of Evening*, which does begin in a very typical Anne Enright opening, goes on to say that over the subsequent—is it twenty-two now, books: novels and collections of short stories?

O'Brien: Well it's like one's age: one loses count, but I think yes.

Patterson: But over those books it became apparent what was actually remarkable about your writing and what had been remarkable from the start had not been sex, but honesty.

O'Brien: Oh!

Patterson: That's what she said. And I suppose when I was talking about that morality, that pursuit, that however it's going to be perceived, as the writer in all of your works you have gone where the writing has taken you at whatever cost.

O'Brien: Yes, as I say, I love magic, but I can't bear dishonesty. I think the books that move me and that I continue to reread are the ones that strip— that just *strip*—away at all the subterfuge and external. Oh yes, it can lure the reader in, as all the great fairy tales do, the Grimm Brothers, I think were greatest writers—not the greatest ever, but in the great echelon. And it's to get to that core, to get to the deepest place that those characters or that story can bring one. And I get quite a few letters from strangers—both the kindness and, a lot of the times, the unkindness, of strangers—and I notice that with a lot of letters I do get, and I am very thankful for them, they are from people, individuals, in a particular and heightened state; sometimes a bereavement, or illness, or fear or in another country, or whatever. And when I have read these things, I think I would be very lonely on Earth, I may be lonely on Earth anyhow, I would be much lonelier on Earth if I didn't have books to read, and books to reread.

And it seems to me that writing—art—does many things; it amuses, it entertains, it enchants, it alters—to some extent—thinking, but what it does above all else is to touch the deepest, truest place of, for want of another word, I have to call the soul. And that, I think, is what many people who read, or who come today to this whole day event, want; either to receive or to give. And it's that mute, but nevertheless mutual, transaction, that makes us continue to read in a world where literature, as you know as well as I do, is sidelined.

The world is raucous. The world is rackety. The world is full of television, noise, music; and reading and staying with the work is a very disciplined and holy occupation. Sartre said once, and I know what he meant—James Joyce would certainly object—but Sartre said that to read a book was to write it. And I think what he meant was that journey that, as readers, we make into a book, it is as if we are composing those very words while we are reading them.

Patterson: We started with *The Country Girls* and, of course, *Madame Cassandra*, and your most recent novel in a way goes back to where you began. It's also dedicated to your mother and your motherland, and has a writer going back to her hometown and her mother.

O'Brien: I'd like to say of my mother, for all her objections of words, she wrote the most fluent, all-consuming letters, and I got them every day. Trunks of them.

[Interview concludes with a reading from *The Light of Evening*]

Edna O'Brien

Mark Lawson / 2009

Reprinted by Permission. Lawson, Mark. "Edna O'Brien." *Front Row*. BBC Radio 4. 11 May 2009. Copyright © "Front Row" BBC Radio 4.

Next year marks the fiftieth anniversary of the publication of *The Country Girls*, the first part of Edna O'Brien's trilogy about rural Ireland's uncertain emergence into the modern world. This and other novels, including *A Pagan Place*, delighted literary critics but infuriated priests because of their sexual frankness. Catholic clergy of the time were discouraged from attending theaters so would not have known about O'Brien's parallel career as a dramatist which continues this week with the premiere in Manchester of *Haunted*, in which a married couple and a young woman reflect on their lives, and perhaps beyond them.

When we met, Edna O'Brien explained that though she continues to write plays and novels, it is much easier to get her books before the public. Theaters often seem concerned that she started writing five decades ago:

O'Brien: I have nothing, let me swear, against young people. I am a mother and grandmother; but there is this notion—or fashion, probably more than notion—that a play by a young person is somehow more acceptable and, that awful word, more trendy or contemporary. That's not necessarily the case. It should not matter either the age, the sex, or the race: it should really be the work. And some theater managements have this very rigid agenda. It is also harder for a woman to get a play on. So the obstacles are considerable and I believe and know that *Haunted*, the reason it's on, even though the director, who is also the manager, Bram Murray of the Royal Exchange loves the play—I know he does—but it was brought to him by the actress Brenda

Blethyn. And had I sent it to him in the proverbial brown envelope, it might not have been opened; but Brenda loved it, finally—

Mark Lawson: And it helps that she had won an Oscar, I imagine they listen to her, do they?

O'Brien: Of course, and she had worked there last year on *The Glass Menagerie.*

Lawson: And on that question, before we talk about *Haunted*, of how few women playwrights there have been historically—very peculiar this, because perhaps the two greatest novelists in the English language have been women, but in the theater they've been very, very sparse until recently.

O'Brien: Yes, they mustn't love the theater or have the same zest for it. I mean, writing for the theater, as I've said in the program note, is a completely different method and metier. When I sit down to write a play, this play, or any play, I imagine the place, the space, and into that space I want to bring the people. Whereas if I sit down to write a novel, gestate or whatever, it's that spell of language, first lines, paragraph that leads me into it, and maybe women writers, since you asked me the question, maybe it is to do with, perhaps, a fear—which is very valid, we all have fear—but also, maybe, not as much a love of theater. When I was young in County Clare, the greatest excitement I ever experienced were tinpot traveling players, overacting, over-pancake-make-upped with their paraffin lamps for headlights, coming once, or, at great luck, twice a year. They put on melodramas, you know *East Lynne, Murder in the Old Red Barn*, but God, was I enraptured! And so was everyone: farmers, men and women, because it brought a world that we'd never heard of before. And that instilled in me, from the very early age, the magic of theater.

Lawson: I was going to ask you about the plays you'd seen growing up because there's a huge love of theater revealed in *Haunted*. The characters at various points talk about plays. They talk about Edward Albee's *Zoo Story*, they discuss a lot of Shakespeare, but growing up, as you famously, even notoriously, did in Catholic Ireland, it must have been quite heavily censored theater, was it?

O'Brien: What's that phrase of Elinor Glyn's? She said, "My heroines never crossed the bedroom door." So nothing crossed the bedroom door, but they were emotional. But I also read and learned off by heart, spouting in fact, in the fields, around the home the speeches of Shakespeare. They were just so extraordinary. It's very funny, in my convent the play we were allowed to do extracts from for the Christmas fête was *Julius Caesar*, and I think it's because there's no sex in *Julius Caesar*. So I know "Friends, Romans, Countrymen" all by heart.

Lawson: The other Shakespeare would be bowdlerized, wouldn't it at that time, you'd be reading at school, I see?
O'Brien: Ah, yes. It wouldn't have been allowed, but sometimes you found a copy of Shakespeare.

Lawson: There are also, I think, clear allusions to Samuel Beckett. The final stage direction doesn't give too much way as footfalls are heard offstage and Beckett wrote a play called *Footfalls*.
O'Brien: I know it well.

Lawson: He has influenced you a lot, I think.
O'Brien: Very much. I love Samuel Beckett's work. I revere it. *Endgame* and *Embers*, to me, are the two greatest plays I've seen or read in my life. It seems a little conceited but, again, I don't wish to be, I knew Samuel Beckett, and he was great company. By great I mean he was so receptive, and a very graceful man. And he hated any talk of literature. It's like when James Joyce said once, he said, "Don't talk to me about literature, talk to me about turnips." But that doesn't mean, that of course, they weren't day and night at their work.

Lawson: If Joyce wanted to talk about turnips, what did you talk to Beckett about? Vegetables, or not?
O'Brien: Oh, many things! A lot about Ireland, because although he had exiled himself, he was still hooked, if you like. His mother had a very, very strong influence on him and both the fear and the love, I would say, would be the word that she engendered in him. We talked about drink as well, all the normal things.

Lawson: I know that some writers, for example the late Harold Pinter—it's hard to get used to saying the late Harold Pinter—he used to send his plays to Beckett, but did you send him manuscripts?

O'Brien: No I didn't. But then Harold sent me—and all his friends—a poem or a play. It's not that I don't want to, for some reason . . . well, maybe I don't want to.

Lawson: The great thing that has changed in your writing career is the freedom you have. There are all these legends of the censorship you suffered early on, of priests burning *The Country Girls* in the parish garden and your mother going through a book and inking out the offending words. I've always wanted to ask you this, but I've never interviewed you before, but did it have any effect on you as a writer? Did you start self-censoring because of what was happening?

O'Brien: It had an effect, but not of self-censorship, because I think at heart, I'm rebellious about the writing and will answer to no one. Otherwise I would have stopped or I'd have been silenced. In the human zone it had, of course, I was very hurt and I was frightened. Who wouldn't be? Because to write at all takes ages. To write a novel takes years. And a play takes at least half a year or a bit more. And you don't do it out of wanting to humiliate or mock a landscape or a family or an event, you do it out of a sort of deep and mysterious involvement. And passion. And love for that place or those characters. For someone to come along then and tell you that you've betrayed them all or whatever or that you shouldn't do it is very disquieting. So on that level, I was hurt. And I avoided them as much as I could because you need freedom to write. You don't want someone to tap on your shoulder.

But as regards freedom with the work itself, let's say the language, ignoring who might or might not read it, the freedom came, I think, from a life really of ongoing reading, because reading is the great education—well, re-reading is the great education. And therefore, I feel although people prefer *The Country Girls* to my last novel, *The Light of Evening*, I don't, but a lot of people do. Freedom came because of having the access to this great galaxy of language in the world and of reading different authors, European authors, English, Irish, American, African, it doesn't matter where, and learning. You learn from everything you read. It's like a gallop of an animal, it just sets you on course. That's, I'm telling you, the good bit. The bad bit is you sit there and the words that come out are creakingly awful which also happens.

Lawson: You were in Ireland last week because they gave you an award. Are you at peace with Ireland, now? You had a hard time for a while.

O'Brien: I know I had a hard time, but that, perhaps, is the school of life.

I am, indeed, delighted to get the award. Seamus Heaney presented it and spent weeks writing this thing. I said, "Oh Seamus, I'm sorry. I wasn't the one who asked you." I was, as I said earlier, nervous by how cross they were with me and how judgmental they were with me for my earlier works. Even though I can kind of understand it. But I never did not love—love is a very, as we know, complicated cake of bread, it includes qualifications, but Ireland has always mattered to me so much. Firstly, because I am Irish, so I couldn't be anything else. But secondly, I was blessed with where I come from, in terms of imagery, in terms of story, in terms of mythic history apart from any other kind of history. It is a very rich place. A rich locale. And were I to deny that—I wouldn't deny it. I wouldn't. So Ireland will always be my motherhood, both in a literary sense and in spiritual sense.

The Troubles with Edna

Jane Hardy / 2010

From *Belfast Telegraph*, 16 February 2010: 22. Copyright © *Belfast Telegraph*. Reprinted by permission.

Her first book, *The Country Girls*, shocked many in Ireland and, as Jane Hardy finds out, Edna O'Brien, whose new play is on in Belfast this week, is still every bit as controversial.

The voice on the phone has a west of Ireland accent, is low in a manner that suggests cigarettes or sensuality, and belongs to the most famous female Irish writer of the last fifty years. In other words, Edna O'Brien.

Plato wrote that poets and storytellers should be banned from his Republic because of their tendency to disseminate dangerous information. In a way, Edna is proud to be a troublemaker if not entirely happy that she has been regarded as a thorn in the side of aspects of the Irish establishment since her first novel, *The Country Girls*, reached an unsuspecting public in 1960.

Its depiction of a rural and, in some ways, backward society which forces heroine Caithleen Brady and her best friend Baba to rebel against their convent upbringing and escape to Dublin, where they are introduced to the ways of the world, was considered shocking.

There are, after all, some fairly explicit scenes, including one moment when Mr. Gentleman, the older man in Caithleen's life, gives her an unsentimental education in sex.

The Irish reaction was instant and disapproving, from Dublin to Tuamgraney, the village in County Clare where Edna grew up. One church demanded members of the congregation hand in their copies for a public burning. She says now, with wry understatement: "It made a little hubbub in its time and I was accused by all sorts of people, including Charles Haughey and the Archbishop of Dublin, of wickedness. Laughable, really, but it did hurt me. But the main thing I was worried about was my mother's reaction—I was terrified of what she would say."

The other aspect of people's obsession with Edna's major bestseller that she dislikes, in spite of the fact that Country Girls became a moneymaking film and a trilogy, is the sense of being defined by it.

"When people say they know my writing and I ask them which books they've read, they always say The Country Girls. I suppose I should be glad that they've read anything."

Her latest work, Haunted, opened last night at the Grand Opera House, Belfast, and the author will be on tour with it. Its chief characters, Mr. and Mrs. Berry, who find themselves on the sharp edges of an emotional triangle, originally appeared in one of six TV plays that Edna O'Brien wrote in the 1960s.

"Well, there are only so many stories in the world and a writer has to think up new devices," she says.

"But Haunted is alive and fresh and new. It's a memory play seen through Mr. Berry's memories of his wife and Hazel."

Clothes are significant in the drama, as Mr. Berry woos the younger woman with outfits removed from his wife's extensive wardrobe. "Yes, clothes are important. I included this detail partly because all women love clothes, but also because Hazel's work is running a vintage clothes stall at World's End down the end of the Kings' Road."

Famously glamorous, Edna O'Brien reveals that in English literary circles her beauty hasn't always worked to her advantage. "If you have, let's say, less than awful looks, it can generate spite as I found when I first came over. It's absurd . . ."

Ms. O'Brien is still able to shock and retains strong views about Ireland, the country she still regards as hers after five decades living in Chelsea, London's grandest postcode.

She has, like everyone else, been following the recent moves on the board as the DUP and Sinn Fein struggled to negotiate an agreement over the devolution of justice and policing from London to Stormont.

Edna says: "Although I am not privy to government thinking I think it's right that the English government should get involved. Although Mrs. Thatcher sent people to their deaths, this government, despite obvious failures elsewhere, is playing equal broker and has been as fair to nationalists as unionists."

She goes on to say that in her view the unionist politicians didn't seem to be supporting the joint position. "Although I have only met a few unionists, intransigence is in their DNA—it's in their history and geography.

"I don't want to sound off but there is on their part a reluctance to concede anything, an ingrained sense of superiority."

Edna, who conducted a notorious interview with former INLA leader Dominic McGlinchey in the early 1990s as background to her novel, *House of Splendid Isolation*, still likes to be controversial.

Like many, she feels that Ireland should be one country, but unlike the majority, she also thinks that there is some justification for the republican armed struggle.

"I feel there was a justification, yes, and I believe Ireland is one country, but my human side is relieved that the guerrilla war, conducted by the UDA and the UVF as well as the IRA, is over. The war is over, congratulations on that."

Although the novelist is approaching eighty, she has no intention of giving up the writing habit that has kept her in the public eye for the last five decades.

She explains: "I've never stopped writing, it's in my heart and is the way I've made my living. I educated my children quite grandly through my writing." Edna laughs.

Her sons Sasha, an architect, and author and *Belfast Telegraph*'s Weekend magazine columnist Carlo Gebler both went to the progressive English boarding school, Bedales.

With passion, their mother adds: "Being a writer is not a romp, but I would continue even if overnight I fell into a fortune."

Recently, Edna has been working on a book that is bound to contain incident, emotion, and enough passages to provide something sensational to read on the train—her autobiography. So does she write a certain amount every day like Graham Greene, who famously produced five hundred impeccable words each morning? She produces a nice anecdote. "Graham told me that when we met in Paris. He took me out for dinner one evening and was very nervous. There was no enmity, but we didn't have a laugh. He couldn't have a drink because of some medication which cast a bit of a pall over things."

So that episode won't feature largely in the O'Brien memoir. Edna won't reveal which passage of her eventful life she's committing to paper first, but says she has written about 25,000 words over the past few days and is tired.

"I write by hand, using violet Zig pens I get in New York. I'm not writing my life story chronologically, although it will be published in sequence. I'm starting with the urgent, vivid passages."

Faber will be publishing the autobiography, whose provisional title is *The Country Girl*.

Edna has known most of the literary great and good in the UK and elsewhere, from Philip Roth to Harold Pinter. On the playwright who died before Christmas, she says: "He was a great friend for forty years, I will miss him. Harold was an individual voice and a very arresting person."

Reading is part of her writer's discipline. "It's like an athlete warming up—I read a scene or so of Shakespeare before I start work. It's so rich and complex. When people say Shakespeare isn't Shakespeare but Marlowe or someone, I think it's a load of cod."

Her reading list is catholic with a small c. "I love reading and reread Samuel Beckett whom I revere. Also Joyce, the nineteenth-century Russians for feeling, including Chekhov—they seem almost Irish. And poetry."

If the woman who memorably described *Mother Ireland* in her 1976 memoir as woman, womb, cave, cow, rosaleen, sow, bride, harlot, and "the gaunt hag of beare" were starting out to write about her homeland now, would she do it differently?

"There are two different things, the portrait of a land and the psyche of a land," she says. "But the situations and feelings would still be true."

On aging, Edna is brisk, saying that she doesn't appreciate what is happening to her joints but that there are benefits.

"The heart is more open, although some would dispute that, and I'm more tolerant."

Strangely, she notes, her recent work, *Byron in Love*, and the short fiction, "Old Wounds," have been moving and quite sad. "I've got to revive my comic instincts," she says.

One of the benefits of age, of course, is meeting the next generation. Edna's five grandchildren live in Enniskillen with younger son Carlo, which is a source of some regret.

"They're not down the road, but that's life." Her youngest grandson, Euan, had celebrated his twelfth birthday the day before and in the evening he got a phone call from London.

"I am quite an indulgent grandmother. I forgot Euan's birthday until the evening, then phoned him and asked what would he like, short of a motor car."

She offered him a jacket, a jumper, or a watch and he opted for the watch. "So I have to find him a very stylish watch."

She sounds happy. "I thank the gods every day of my life to have been allowed to be a writer."

Edna O'Brien

William Crawley / 2010

From *Out to Lunch with William Crawley*, Queen's University, Belfast, 10 November 2010. Copyright © *Out to Lunch with William Crawley*, Queen's University, Belfast. Reprinted by permission.

William Crawley: Welcome to my front room. I mean, this has now become such a homely space for me, I feel like it's partly mine! Maybe Queen's will mortgage it out to me someday. It is my great pleasure to welcome you to our conversation today and to involve you in the conversation as well, because Edna O'Brien is so many things in one life: a novelist, a short story writer, a playwright, a critic, a historian of language, a biographer, I think I can even throw the word journalist in if you won't shy away from the word journalist as well, will you? Well, we'll see. She is a writer, as simple as that. And she's a writer that's left her mark on the lives of other writers and inspired a new generation of writers that we take for granted in many ways in the post-Joycian period of writing, and she is a writer who has left her mark on Ireland and in her home beyond Ireland; but we'll find out more about that in a minute. For now, please welcome to the stage the one, the only, Edna O'Brien.
Edna O'Brien: Hello.

WC: And you're very welcome to Belfast, and the Great Hall, greater still today.
EO: It's very nice.

WC: Isn't it lovely, isn't it? And I think Prince Charles, when he was opening this, he spotted somebody over there and said, "Is that one of my relatives?" And indeed it was.
EO: Well, Brian Boru might be lurking somewhere out there . . .

WC: Can we start by talking about Belfast, actually? Because, obviously, you're a graduate of this University, an honorary graduate, and I was at your graduation ceremony. I was getting a degree the same day that Edna was getting her honorary doctorate; I remember it very well. And I just wanted to find out, first of all, how do you feel about Belfast and the North of Ireland?

EO: Well, how long have we? A couple of hours? I've been quite often to Belfast, and I do like it. What I find surprising, even in this day and age, people are very, very friendly and actually human. It's a friendlier city, in ways, than Dublin or London. And this morning, I walked around looking for something—a flower shop—and I thought: to live in a city where you're so near the mountains and you feel the sky is a huge thing. I don't know enough to really answer your question thoroughly because I'm a tourist. That's it. Well, I'm Irish. So you would be the person that I should ask that question of. We'll have to get a different question.

WC: Well, you could come for research here, couldn't you, and set a novel in Belfast, in the future?

EO: Well, I suppose I could if there are any ideas.

WC: We'll make some offers by the end of the interview and see where we go with it.

EO: Alright. We'll try it. We'll try it.

WC: This is a big anniversary year for you: not only are you a writer that has continually, prolifically produced new writings, but also you can look back now over fifty years at the landscape of your own work. And this year we're talking a great deal about *The Country Girls*, the fiftieth anniversary of *The Country Girls*.

EO: Yes, and also, I will be eighty years of age, I might as well admit it. I used to take a year or two or three off my age, but you know, people caught up with it.

WC: Wikipedia's terrible for that.

EO: And you're the man that at lunch, my new friend Mr. Crawley, he was eating very decorously and not drinking, and he—I'll tell your story—he can consult Google for how many calories that little cabbage was. So equally, if I said, "Well I'll be seventy-six this year," you could have googled.

WC: I would have checked it. I already have checked it.

EO: So it is a year, but now, looking back is one thing, but one also has to live in the present; and as far as one can, live in a sort of hope in the mad world that we all inhabit to have some little river of hope for the future. And that is, somehow, harder as one gets older. Not just me, but lots of people. Because one gets a little bit more inner, and enclosed. I thank God and my personal history and the County Clare and a few other things, that I could write, *can* write, and hopefully always will write.

Fifty years of *The Country Girls,* as you mentioned. When I started *The Country Girls*, I moved to England. I had that child, he's a grown man over there now, Carlo, and his brother and their father. And I was asked to write this book because I had been writing reader's reports about novels submitted to publishers. And I was given the noble sum of £50. It's not so bad, come to think of it. £50 by an English and American publisher to write a book. I was then, and am now, a little bit extravagant, profligate, even when I don't have it in life. So I spent the £50. I bought my children some ammunition, I deeply disapproved, plastic ammunition. And in order to be, so to speak, to the man I was married to, a good wife, I bought a sewing machine. I have never used a sewing machine and I never intend to use a sewing machine. In short, the book had now to be written.

And I had left Ireland voluntary. In fact, I was glad to have left. And when I sat down, and when Carlo and Sasha were brought to school, at this wide window sill in this little house in S.W.20, it was miles from anywhere—you had to get a bus to get a bus—I sat down to write, and I did not know what I would write. The first words came "I wakened quickly and sat up in bed abruptly. It is only when I am anxious that I waken easily, and then I remember to the old reason: my father had not come home." And that was the start. And literally, this has happened to me nowadays, each day for five or six hours I just wrote this book. And it would be honorable of me to say it was written almost for me by a spirit. I was the messenger. And part of the luck with that situation was that I had left Ireland and home, but I didn't know how deeply home, for better and sometimes painfully, was engraved in me.

It's a fairly funny book, certainly funnier than the books I'm writing now, unfortunately. At least Baba is funny. Although the book had comedy in Baba, you know let's feck about chocolate and all that was, of course, deemed bad. I mean the word. It has a youth in it, the energy is bigger—and to some extent—the defiance of youth.

What I did not foresee was, just as well, that the book would cause a little furor in my own county and, indeed, in my own house. There was no tradition of writers and I wanted to be a writer before I knew what being a writer was. It wasn't written, as was thought, to ridicule or humiliate my own country. Why should I? There are a lot of things that I might not like about my own country, but there are the many things I love about it. It started with a nun from my convent saying, "We hear you have written a novel. We give credence and open mind." Well I didn't like the sound of that. There's credence and *credence* . . .

Then there was the banning, which, as you know, Dublin, Ireland, rather, the south of Ireland, particularly Dublin, they were wizards about banning! They were inverse magicians! They were nameless. I can't say they were blameless, but no one knew who they were. And the banning—anybody could have a book banned. Even using an anonymous name, you could pick three lines and send it in. So the book was banned. And that was way beyond me. I mean, I didn't mind . . . I mean I minded, but I didn't mind.

WC: You'd love to get a book banned now, wouldn't you?

EO: Well, exactly! At that time, Myles na Gopaleen wrote a little column, and you know how witty he was, and he said, "Oh that cute one from the turnips!" Because he was always talking about turnips. He wished that he was banned. But my mother was very upset about it. There was a little burning of a book or two at the chapel grounds. And I've said this before, but I'll say it because, maybe, someone didn't know: my mother, naturally, told me about it, she said women fainted. And I said, well maybe turf smoke? And my mother did something that I don't think she'd do now, but I mention it not to accuse the dead, but to give some sense of what the culture and the society and the world was in County Clare and Ireland and possibly here as well in 1960, she had taken a pen with black ink and had inked out every offending word in the book. I found the book in a bolster case after my mother had died. I was so angry. I was so angry. And what I think now is, my God, how frightened she must have been by that work, which is really two girls bursting for life. But what I came on a bit later—and then I'll stop, I was just warming up—was the august correspondence between Charles Haughey who was the Minister of Culture—and something else, you know they doubled up in those days—

WC: Culture of Money, I think.

EO: And Archbishop McQuaid, and the Archbishop of Westminster. Little did I know that letters flowed between these hypocrites, if you want the true word. I was going to say big men. And they all deemed that the book should not be in the hands of any household. That it was, as it was said in the pa-

pers, "a smear on Irish womanhood." I look back on it and I think, because
I sometimes get requests from students, in fact, one the other day from
Dublin that I think Carlo teaches, she asked me a rather innocent question:
"Would I have written the book if I had known it was going to be banned
and cause such a brouhaha?" And I wrote back and said I would have written the book, but I didn't think about things like that. When you sit down to
write, and I'm sure there are writers here, you cannot think who will like or
dislike or hate this book. Philip Roth, my great friend who is full of wit, as an
aside, his wittiest remark was in the paper the other day. Philip said, and you
will like this, "For every reader born now, thirty readers are dying." And he
said to me once, you know Americans, "Kid, who do we write for? No one.
Ourselves." Not in totality, we hope, an egomaniacal, monomaniacal way,
but you have no idea once you let the book or poem or drama out into the
world. And I'm very glad—more than glad—that so many people have come
today. I'm surprised, but I'm delighted.

WC: And it wasn't just banned, it was also burned, wasn't it?
EO: That's the turf smoke, yes.

WC: By the local priests, yeah?
EO: Yes, yes. I think they're a bit ashamed of that now, because I was in
Scariff lately at the library—no library in the past—and that episode is wish-
ing to be forgotten. There was no library, but there was one thing. And it
shows how people, and I hope it will still happen, have a hunger for books,
even if they're not always that keen to buy a book. And in our village, one
woman had managed to get a copy of *Rebecca* by Daphne du Maurier. And
Rebecca! Oh boy did Scariff hop with the passion of *Rebecca*. It was loaned
to hungry readers, but not by the consecutive page, so you got page 104 then
you went back to page 3. Very hard to follow the plot.

Once, I saw another book, which I now possess, and actually think is a
great book. *Dracula* by Bram Stoker. The cover of *Dracula* says, "her lus-
cious lips reached towards him and the two canine teeth" and so on. And
Dracula I saw—twice a year we had traveling players put up by amateur
dramatics. And they'd come into the village and you'd hear about it two
weeks before. Laid out on stone walls underneath a rock would be a buff
poster with *Dracula, East Lynne, Murder in the Old Red Barn*. And they
were my first introduction to theater. I think of any young person, any child,
seeing for the first time something up there, on stage, actors would be taking
tickets at the door all covered in pancake makeup and togas and that. And I

remember *Dracula*, because they did the play of *Dracula*, very shortened, I have to confess, and Dracula had a very large safety pin, which was dragged across the heroines neck and then the fake blood came out.

So I had no education and a very rich education in that I did not go to university. I don't regret it. I know I'm in a very esteemed building, but the thing about writing is, Virginia Woolf said this in a more formal way than I'm about to say it; to write, and keep writing, you have to read and keep reading and rereading. That's your education. Like an athlete's training every day, the rereading of the King James Bible, Shakespeare, James Joyce, Sylvia Plath, Emily Brontë, Chekhov, anyone, as long as they're great. Early in my life, I had no books, but later, when I got access to books, almost when I first got married, I was able to read, if you like, with the dedication and relish—which is a far more important word here—of that of a child or someone who never read. Where if I'd had a formal education, others, professors, would be telling one about a book. And therefore I count myself, in many ways, very lucky in life. However, I haven't been lucky in love and I haven't been lucky with houses. Could I mention those two things? Just so that no one thinks, "Oh her life is so good."

WC: They're almost literary themes, aren't they?
EO: They sure are, they sure are.

WC: You mention Philip Roth. I think he says he writes 365 days of the year, eight hours a day.
EO: He's very monk-like in his ways. He does write a lot. He does keep to himself a lot. He's probably, without exaggeration, the funniest person I have ever met. That high gift of comedy, which is a mix of Groucho Marx and Kafka, but there is nothing without a price. And I am sure that high comedy, indeed I know he has written about this, comes with the downsides and the breakdown once or twice. He is dedicated to literature. And he has introduced me to a lot of books I would never read. I had never read *The Magic Mountain*, and he made me read it. But when I first met him, I used to cook, as Carlo knows, rather extensively for a lot of people. I had this Celtic, still have, but it's getting a little harder as I get older—

WC: I gave you a beet root recipe earlier.
EO: Yes, I had this Celtic notion, that one makes, you know, a feast, a feast or a famine. I always cooked for myself and many people, easily sixty or seventy or a hundred. Crazy. But that was the first time Philip met me, because

Claire Bloom was a friend of mine and she'd been in a film script I wrote. So he came to the house. And one of the things in this world that has often irked me, not you, with him, sometimes, and I'll come back to Philip in one minute, sometimes journalists have come to the house, and often women journalists as well, and have, if you like, interviewed one's hair. And one's fireplace. And they have given, if you like, the caption or emblem of superficiality just because one manages to look half okay. But that night, in my house, Philip was a little condescending. And he made some remark about, oh, did I fit in a bit of writing in between making soup and cooking a goose. And I was rather, I didn't like it. I didn't react. And about a month later he rang me up and said, "I want to come and see you. I'm going to come and see you." And I said that's good. And he had read a book of mine called *Night*. And he knew that the mockery from the first time wasn't fair. And that's to show you he's, what they call in some societies, a midge. But he's also a very formidable man. Very formidable. And huge intelligence. *Huge* intelligence.

WC: Still trying to get a sense of how your imagination was unlocked as a writer to write the first book, because you didn't have the literary training that some writers have in terms of going to university. You studied chemistry in the evening and pharmacy and worked in a shop.
EO: Oh, that was an education. Making suppositories, making emulsions, making worm powder—it's good training for cooking, sorry to mention it.

WC: But what is it that, while you're in London, what is it that frees you to start writing? Surely it's not just the pressure of a £50 advance, is it?
EO: No, it's in one, I think, even before one even knows what words are. I seem to be name dropping, and I promise, I'm not, certain writers I've had a chance to talk with. The great Samuel Beckett would not disagree, with whom I met and liked and admired more than any writer. I reread Samuel Beckett the way I would read prayer. And not just read it, feel it. I think that all the writers that I have met, and I have met many, some pretty awful to tell you the truth. Well, you know conceited and so on, and some not. But reading the diaries of writers, the letters of writers—Faulkner, Chekhov— this thing inside one, nothing to do with mother, father, relatives, anything. Samuel Beckett put it brilliantly to a preface to Jack Yeats's drawings which were in a little book, and he said the artist who stakes his life has no brother and comes from nowhere. And actually, there's a great truth in that. You do come from somewhere, and you have a great deal of people, blood relatives and such who don't like what you write, but that's another casualty of the

work. I think it is a longing that can never actually be fulfilled: to get to the truth and the pith and the everythingness of life and human interaction. Kafka put it, great literature should take an axe to the frozen heart. Now that's a tall order. However, that's a great tall order.

Naturally when I started out with just with these little words, these words that I was mad about, I didn't know about the axe to the frozen heart, what I think I knew was that I had a longing, and more than a longing, a determination. Because you have to have a determination to do it and keep doing it no matter what, no matter who doesn't like you, no matter what, that's your agenda; and one has to, and it doesn't always make you the nicest or most accommodating person. Well, too bad. You have to do it. But I felt my own little world. And, indeed, my world is circumscribed. I don't know big worlds. I don't know what's happening to people who live in awful camps. I don't know what's happening to women in Muslim countries married at the age of twelve. I read about these things, I see them on television, as we all do. I am very aware of the enormity of the world around me and unfortunately, the limitation of my own scope; my experience, my situation, etc. But what I do know, or have to keep knowing, have to keep believing is that if, in my own way, I can deliver, somehow, a little record of my own experience, that someone else, that you or she, or him or her, will identify with and that's all I can do. And the only way I can do that is with the words. But it's not just the words, as Joyce put it so simply, he said, "I have all the words, it's a question of how to put those words together." And it's the intensity—intensity is a much mocked feeling and emotion. I detest a word that people use a lot, be *cool*. Why be cool when life is full of passion? Of love and hate and murders and marriages and dramas. Cool? Cool is for a drink. A soft drink, even. So that was my remains. My burning, burning feeling.

WC: Sometimes when people try to describe your work, certain words repeat themselves in discussions like "romantic love" and "passion," but there is an immense disappointment and loss within your work.
EO: And fury.

WC: And fury. And I read someone the other day, people can say very cruel things about you as a writer. Someone described you the other day as the inventoress of Chick Lit. It seemed to me that was such a disparaging thing to say.
EO: Who is this person, let's get them in here. Get your Google out!

WC: It seems to me, the difference between you and Chick Lit is the difference between advertising copy and poetry. There is a lyricism and a respect for language that is not always evident in romantic writings of that kind, but is very evident in your writing.

EO: Oh, I love this. You're going to have to get the Chick Lit person. I tell you. I like this question, and we'll talk about what romantic really is in a little bit, but the other week or so I was in Galway at a festival, and afterwards there was a bit of chatting and a nun, she said "I have kept this paper clipping for forty years hoping I'd meet you." So I take the paper clipping and I think this is going to be lovely, and I'm back in the hotel that evening having a little glass of wine and I get the clipping out. . . . Oh my god! Savagery including "Edna O'Brien is the bargain basement Molly Bloom." Well, you know something, it's a good thing I'm not armed. I think it's so easy to have a cheap shot at someone. And also the kind of books I write, some people love reading them, some people don't. Because, again, they're intense. I think if I were a man, or if I had taken, as the poor Brontë sisters had to do, a male pseudonym, let's say I called myself Edmund O'Brien, they wouldn't talk of Chick Lit or whatever bargain basement. It's less and less, but there has been a relegation of such, a dismissal and a scorn of women writers or women artists. So that is one of the things you have to take, but not take lying down.

As regards to your question, William, of romantic, I think, in life, I have been a little romantically unwise. I don't think my fiction or my plays are romantic. They're full of yearning. They're full of misplaced emotions and passions. They're full of love, rejected love, unrealized love, but that isn't romantic as the word has tended to be cheapened. And one of the things about being a writer, one of the many things, is one has to take all of the ugly things and somehow keep going. Byron, on whom I wrote a short book last year called *Byron in Love*, put it very sensibly, except, of course, he only applied it to men. In a letter to Shelley he said, "A man should calculate on his powers of resistance before entering the literary life." And it's very, very true.

Every job you have to have the power of resistance, but the trouble with the writer and being attacked is the writing itself is so hard. The finding it is truly like digging for gold. And when a story, or even a little paragraph comes to one, it comes with hard work and rewriting and rewriting, but it comes as a little miracle to the doer. Now to get attacked for that is very hard going, plus the fact that you might wobble or have the old self-doubt. And then sit down the next morning and start the next page. That is, I think, one of the hardest things about writing, the ongoing have to keep doing it.

And have to hope that it will come. Like, at the moment I have a collection of short stories, *Saints and Sinners*—

WC: Listen up for the book program for next year.
EO: Yes, this is for next year. And I'm supposed to be writing a memoir and it's causing me unwarranted—no, not unwarranted, unspeakable—anxiety and fear and hesitation and all the usual things, only worse. And I dream at night of this. It's only a book after all, I saw a sign once on a wall in London—two signs—it says, and this is outside a football grounds in Fulham, one said, "Kierkegaard Rule o.k."—as if anyone knew what that was—and the other said, "Rock n Roll o.k." It's only a book, okay, but it inhabits and engrosses every waking and sleeping moment of my life. And one dream, recurring—I write by hands and by pen. Even today I had to wash off a bit of the old ink because pens leak on an airplane. Someone should invent pens that don't leak on an airplane—I was dreaming I had written pages on this manuscript on white foolscap with purple ink, but all the words had slid into one another. So when I'd wakened, I wasn't exactly confident. Should we talk of funny things now? I'm boring them.

WC: Would you be a writer had you stayed in Ireland?
EO: I think I might have been in and out of a lunatic asylum, some of the time. In 1958 is when I actually left Ireland. The book came out in 1960. I wrote it in the three weeks of Christmas in 1958 and the beginning of 1959. I wrote with great pain and great sorrow and a lot of vitality, as well, but I wrote in total ignorance. I didn't think of my mother or the parish priest or the woman in the post office who said I should be kicked naked through the town, she said to my father. I wondered why naked? Why not fully dressed? I didn't think of any of that. Thank God, nor couldn't.

If I had stayed in Ireland at that time and the book came out and there was a lot of commotion about it. And a lot of wild, heated things said and said to me and anonymous letters about sewage, sinking in my own sewage, you know. It's nothing compared to Russia where people are sent to a gulag. It's nothing. And I again want to stress that, but at the same time, it wasn't exactly a birthday party for me. If I had stayed, then I might have been more frightened to pick up my pen to write the next book and the next. Ireland has fed me and continues to do so in all sorts of ways. First of all, temperament. I write in the English language, but I'm an Irish writer, my temperament is that particular. Secondly, that particular kind of language. Thirdly, I come from a place, a parish, a field around home, Dewsboro, that house, that has a most ongoing, if you like, pathological indelible effect on me. It's the actualities, the ghosts of that place, the feelings put in me that are still there. Feelings of fear, I was very frightened as a child. And also full of a kind of baffled wonder. I felt there were some marvelous things, but I didn't know what they were. And the fear was fear of many things. Fear of God, which was a fear of church. Fear of parents. It was a world of constant subjugation and people watching. So one's little sins—or big sins or whatever they were—felt more enormous because of this overall watching. And this was from all sides. What I forgot, or failed to notice, was they were being watched too. So Ireland has given me a big casket.

WC: You wouldn't mind the moral surveillance without the hypocrisy, though. The hypocrisy makes the moral surveillance particularly galling.
EO: I hate hypocrisy. It abounds. Not just the Irish. Every country. It's a big disguise. I was reading, as I said to you at lunch today, George Bush, who is now the white-haired boy again. I promised not to talk about politics, but I have to bring this in. He's the white-haired man, in the best sense of the word, of the Republican Party again, and he says that water boarding and torture and everything in the prison at Guantanamo actually stopped terrorist actions. But British Intelligence, and if you'd like, they're on the same side—Britain and the U.S.A.—about the war in Iraq and other terrible catastrophes, even British Intelligence has disputed it. Now that is not only hypocrisy on the part of George Bush, it's total lies. And a chutzpah saying, "I am a great guy who prevented deaths." That's not the truth. That is it on a huge global and catastrophic scale. But in our own lives, too, I often think of people I know and I like and yet in social situations behave a little differently. Where a little bit of the posh of hypocrisy comes in.

WC: Yeah, and then they pop out and do a little water boarding in the back when you're not looking. You mention Joyce a lot and Beckett. Joyce said that Ireland is the old sow that eats her farrow.
EO: Yes, he felt it.

WC: Do you feel that way too? Do you feel eaten up and spat out?
EO: Well, it's not all spat out. It's written out in beautiful prose. I think Joyce, like Beckett, are very divided about Ireland. Joyce's childhood—everyone has read Richard Ellman's book and then I wrote a book about Joyce. I loved Richard Ellman and his book. Joyce, for a man to come from a family so poor, flitting from house to house overnight. A sparring father. A drinking

father. A man who said to his wife, "You've given birth to thirteen children, die and be done with it." That's not exactly happy family time. He had tremendous obstacles and hated suffocation and hypocrisy and jurisdiction of Mother Church. Nevertheless, he was extremely influenced by it. His piece on the fires of hell and purgatory, those pages of *Portrait*, oh boy, no Jesuit could do them as well. I mean they're fantastic. So he was very influenced by his upbringing and his church and he said one of the three greatest influences in his life was his mother's kiss, the holy host on his tongue—holy communion—and a prostitute's lingual kiss. They were the three things that mixed in. For the writer, you need conflict. You don't write out of a happy place. You don't write because you're making jam. Nothing wrong with making jam, but you have to have conflict. He had it a plenty.

WC: Sort of birth, marriage, and death, he's describing. Isn't it?

EO: His intelligence for language was something phenomenal. Giant. On every level: scatological, religious, emotional. He broke language. It's like he discovered the atomic bomb. So he could not have remained in Ireland, and when he left, they said he could have had a good job on the *Irish Independent* as a reporter, but I don't think that would have suited him. So he was very cruel and offensive about Ireland, including saying she was the sow that eats her farrow. And so was Beckett, who, as you know, revered James Joyce at first and went so far as to wear the shoes, that didn't fit him, the same as Joyce's shoes and smoked in the same way Joyce did.

But it's a complicated thing. It's both wanting to be back in the womb of the land or the actual mother or the archetypal mother. To be back at where the first source of—for want of a better word I'll say—inspiration occurred and the reasons for it and also to flee that land, flee that mother, flee that suffocation. And it's that dichotomy, that crisis, that contradiction in the self and in those two gigantic authors that created such lasting work. Because when you think of it ultimately, when you think of Beckett's plays, sure, they're funny. But what's the greatest thing about them? They touch the human person. They touch the soul, as deep as you can get. It's a cry for night, now weep in darkness. There's no less hope.

But [Beckett] was a very funny man as well. I once visited him in his area of Paris where he lived just towards the end of his life and we discussed graveyards. He was very surprised that I have a graveyard in Ireland. He was very disapproving—but that's another story. I go up to this hotel called the Pullman Hotel where there were busloads of people and their luggage and so on. And to give you a little idea of the man he was, he was, of course, a great intellect, but he had a childlikeness still in him. And he said, "Edna, do you think the air is gray up here?" It was awful. It's the same air as anywhere else. But somebody else, I was in Paris recently, I had a book come out, and somebody told me, whenever they were out walking, they always saw Beckett walking. He walked the streets of Paris, and yet he wrote—he didn't call it Dublin—but he wrote about Ireland. So Ireland was quite a fount to come from.

WC: It's a bit of a haunting, isn't it?
EO: It's more than a haunting. It's—what's the thing you said that vampires do? What's the word along with haunting? It sucks one's blood, I suppose. And that's both disturbing and fertilizing.

WC: A lot of the language you use to describe inspiration and the writing of it seems religious. You know, the miracle moment, the spirit almost giving it to you. Would you say you're particularly religious?
EO: I'd say I sort of am, to tell you the truth.

WC: You don't share that with Joyce and Beckett.
EO: Joyce asked for a priest on his deathbed and the priest refused to give absolution. There are two different things. There is God and the idea of God, and the Holy Ghost with the forty tongues and the gift of the tongues. There's that, what shall we call it, unproven, but nevertheless search for that thing. Nietzsche put it, if God didn't exist then man would have to invent him. Very true remark. That is a spiritual quality, a spiritual ingredient in people, whoever, or whatever version of God that person carries. And then there is the Church. And, if you like—no, not if you like—it's a fact. I don't know anything about the Muslim religion and their clerics, but if you read the Catholic Church and the cruelty of the Catholic Church down the centuries and the inquisition. I mean, when I told my mother that Popes had married—i.e., the Borgias had married. She was pounding potatoes and I thought she'd kill me with the pounder. So the actual politics of the church ongoingly is quite different to the longing for, search for, finding of true faith. They're different things. Now the Church won't agree. If the Pope was here today, he'd strongly disagree with me, but I would also disagree with him. So I find it, therefore, and I've used the term several times before, a split in one.

I want a sense of God, we all do. I'm not being sentimental. I want the help of God, if that is possible, but I cannot accept—and it's not that I want to be wayward, I'm not suggesting that—some of the teachings and tenets of the Catholic Church are very hard. If I were or you were a woman in a poor part of South America where he went, Pope John Paul II, and said that contraception was a mortal sin, and I had thirteen children, and I still wanted to feel close to God, that's not good, is it? Every religion is dogmatic. And every religious teacher is dogmatic, because they have to be. In their own way, they're as dogmatic as Stalin was. Communism was a religion. A secular religion. So that what I am asking in a world where people love a control over other people and are judgmental. I'm asking to allow that the spirit be free. It's a tall order.

WC: Well, You brought a few things up with George Bush. Let me ask you a few things about the border here in Ireland and whether it's as written in bold as it once was? Is it fading out? Is there more of a connectedness between the two parts of this island today?
EO: Absolutely. You know that, you live here. Oh, absolutely. And I know it.

WC: More understanding across the border, perhaps?
EO: I think understanding in theory and understanding in life are two different things, but at least there is a commencement. There is. I'll tell you a story, it's not about now, but it's relevant. I wrote a book called *House of Splendid Isolation* which was a man in the North, a guerrilla fighter part of whatever group, IRA, INLA, it doesn't matter. That nationalist fighter, it was about him going to the south and finding that people in the South were as against him as in the North. I was researching this book, not as a tourist to your fine province, but as someone from the South having read about all the murders on all the sides, the carnage, the tragedy. I was very aware of them.

I met a man down in County Clare who had shot an IRA man on the day of a robbery at a post office. The robbery went wrong. The woman in the post office had taken up a gun. So the two men fled and the guard was called about four miles from where I come and there was a shootout on the road just near a place called Feakle. And I went to see the guard to talk to him and I said, what was it like, Albert. And it was full John Wayne, he had gotten out of the car and quick movie time. And I said, what did you feel Albert, when he was left with the dead body? He said, when you're shooting, it's 50/50—he's from Cork, Albert—but when you shot him dead, it's a different thing, because we're all Irish, under the skin. I thought that was an extraordinary profound remark. Not just a remark, a statement. So that was my trigger for coming. That was now . . . twenty years ago. And as we all know things are better now. And they will be better still.

When I was researching, I remember going to Long Kesh and talking to Protestants and Catholics and actually people in prison are dying to talk to you. I remember talking to a Protestant boy whose name I don't know, but I remember the conversation very well. And he told me that one Christmas he was in the infirmary. And I just give you this one thing, this tiny example. But tiny things are what happen to make bigger things happen. He was in the infirmary and they were a bit short of staff, it being Christmas day. So Catholic and Protestant were near each other. And this was the first time he had genuinely, truly ever spoken to a Catholic in there or even before he went in. He said, "I couldn't believe that," he said, "that the guy didn't have two horns." And he meant that. He wasn't being ugly or radical. It's these innate beliefs people have, whether it's here or in Iraq between Sunnis, it's this innate belief that is fed to them by their rulers on whatever side, and fed by the climate and ferment of hatred to believe the worst. And when you say to me this, I—of course there is change; of course there is room for a lot more change. And in its way, although art may seem a luxury or elitist, and some people think it is, I don't think it is. I think it as necessary as breathing.

Art can bridge some gap, so can sport, between people of different divides. There is that and there is time; time in which it is very hard for people on either side to forget, or to forgive. It is very hard to forgive terrible things, but they have to. They have to—it's not that they forget them, they have to know what that war was and why that war. *Why?* Why did you have to have British soldiers on these streets? You have to go back and back. And I can well see that somebody sitting alone would say, "Well you see my son or my daughter . . . " and describing it to me. And I can well see how the horror of that never ever passes, but it is to find some reasonableness and equanimity. The fuelers of hatred are people that I blame.

Are we finished?

WC: We could go on forever, what are you talking about! And we may well.
EO: I have no idea. I don't want to keep anyone, but I do want to say, you've been very nice to me and to tell you in the audience, that sitting at the lunch I was a bit shaky, a bit nervy, and I said William, do you think you could tell me the first question? And he said, I have no idea what it is.

Key Resources

Anderson, Susan. "For Edna O'Brien, Writing Is a Kind of Illness." *New York Times.* 11 October 1977.

Battersby, Eileen. "Life of O'Brien." *Irish Times.* 14 October 1999: 29.

Bell, Geoffrey. "Without Bitterness: An Interview with Edna O'Brien." *Fortnight* 47 (1972): 19–20.

Byrne, Gay. *Edna O'Brien. The Meaning of Life.* RTÉ One. 21 February 2010.

Carpenter, Andrew, Seamus Deane, and Jonathan Williams. *The Field Day Anthology of Irish Writing.* Vol. IV/V. Angela Bourke, ed. New York: NYU Press, 2002.

Child, Julia. *Julia Child Presents "Lunch with Edna O'Brien." HUNGRY: The Literary Julia Child.* Audio. Leet and Litwin, ca. 1997. http://www.prx.org/pieces/45301-julia-child-presents-lunch-with-edna-o-brien.

Clarity, James. "At Lunch with Edna O'Brien; Casting a Cold Eye." *New York Times.* 30 August 1995.

Colletta, Lisa, and Maureen O'Connor, eds. *Wild Colonial Girl: Essays on Edna O'Brien.* Madison: University of Wisconsin Press, 2006.

Cooke, Rachel. "Edna O'Brien: 'A Writer's Imaginative Life Commences in Childhood.'" *Observer.* 6 February 2011.

Daiches, David, and Jon Stallworthy, eds. "Edna O'Brien." *The Norton Anthology of English Literature.* Vol. 2. New York: Norton, 1985.

de Vere White, Terence. "The Lady's Not for Burning." *Irish Times.* 12 May 1962.

———. "Talking to Edna O'Brien." *Irish Times.* 12 May 1965: 11.

Donovan, Katie. *Irish Women Writers: Marginalised by Whom?* Dublin: Raven Arts, 1988.

Dunn, Nell. "Edna." *Talking to Women.* London: MacGibbon and Kee, 1965: 69–107.

Eckley, Grace. *Edna O'Brien.* Lewisburg, PA: Bucknell University Press, 1974.

Eliot, T. S. *Introducing James Joyce.* London: Faber and Faber, 1942.

Ellmann, Richard. *James Joyce.* New York: Oxford University Press, USA, 1983.

———, and Charles Feidelson. *The Modern Tradition: Backgrounds of Modern Literature.* New York: Oxford University Press, USA, 1965.

Evenson, Laura. "Edna O'Brien's Haunting Origins." *San Francisco Chronicle.* 10 May 1997.

Gallagher, W. D. "Review of Portrait of the Artist as a Young Girl." *Irish Literary Supplement.* August 1987: 5.

Gilbert, Sandra, and Susan Gubar. *No Man's Land: The Place of the Woman Writer in the Twentieth Century.* New Haven: Yale University Press, 1987.

Gilbert, Stuart. *The Letters of James Joyce,* vol.1. New York: Viking, 1957, rev. 1966.

Joyce, James. *Dubliners.* London: Grant Richards, Ltd., 1914.

———. *Finnegans Wake.* London: Faber and Faber, 1939.

———. *A Portrait of the Artist as a Young Man.* New York: B. W. Huebsch, 1916.

———. *Ulysses.* Paris: Sylvia Beach, 1922.

Kersnowski, Alice. "Edna O'Brien in England and Ireland: 1967-1997." Clare Hall, University of Cambridge. Cambridge, UK. November 1997. Lecture.

———. *Edna O'Brien: The Fourth Net.* (forthcoming).

———. "Edna O'Brien: The Writer and Social Change." International Association for the Study of Irish Literature. ISAIL. University of Limerick, Limerick, Ireland. July 1998. Lecture.

———. "The Fourth Net: Edna O'Brien, An Irish Modernist." Diss. University College Dublin, 1989.

———. "An Irish Classic." *Sewanee Review.* CXIV.3 (Summer 2006): xlvii–xlviii.

———. "Literary Conversations with James Joyce and Edna O'Brien." XXIII International James Joyce Symposium. Trinity College Dublin, June 2012.

Kiberd, Declan. *Inventing Ireland: The Literature of the Modern Nation.* Cambridge: Harvard University Press, 1995: 566.

Laing, Kathryn, Sinéad Mooney, and Maureen O'Connor. *Edna O'Brien: "New Critical Perspectives."* Dublin: Carysfort Press, 2006.

Longley, Edna. "Pilgrim Mothers." *Partisan Review.* 47.2 (1980): 308–13.

Lydon, Christopher. *Edna O'Brien. Open Source.* Public Radio International. 13 October 2006.

McCarthy, Charlie, dir. *Edna O'Brien: Life, Stories.* Prod. Cliona ní Bhuachalla. RTÉ Television. 8 May 2012.

Nicholson, Nigel. "On Edna O'Brien's *Virginia."* *Virginia Woolf Miscellany.* Spring 1981.

O'Brien, Edna. "Why Irish Heroines Don't Have to Be Good Anymore." *New York Times Book Review.* 11 May 1986.

———.   "Ulster's Man of the Dark." *New York Times.* 1 February 1994.

Pearce, Sandra Manoogian. "An Interview with Edna O'Brien." *Canadian Journal of Irish Studies* 22.2 (1996): 5–8.

Rehm, Diane. *Edna O'Brien: "Saints and Sinners."* *The Diane Rehm Show.* NPR. 23 May 2011.

Senn, Fritz. "Reverberations." *James Joyce Quarterly.* Spring 1966: 82–87.

Showalter, Elaine. *A Literature of Their Own: British Women Novelists from Brontë to Lessing.* Princeton: Princeton University Press, 1977.

Walsh, Caroline. "The Return of Edna O'Brien." *Irish Times.* 12 November 1977: 9.

———. "Edna O'Brien: Miles from Melancholy." *Irish Times.* 11 June 1988: 22.

Wolff, Tobias, Dan Griggs, and the Lannan Foundation. *Edna O'Brien in Conversation with Tobias Wolff. Lannan Literary Videos.* Santa Fe: Lannan Foundation, 1999.

Index